Putze
Performances 2000–2020

arnoldsche

Für Lucia, Raphael, Antonia

Ihr habt euren Papa bei allen Höhenflügen nach unten und bei allen Tauchgängen wieder nach oben gebracht; und das tut ihr immer noch.

For Lucia, Raphael, and Antonia

You brought your dad back down to earth from all flights of fancy and brought him back up again whenever he fell—and you continue to do so.

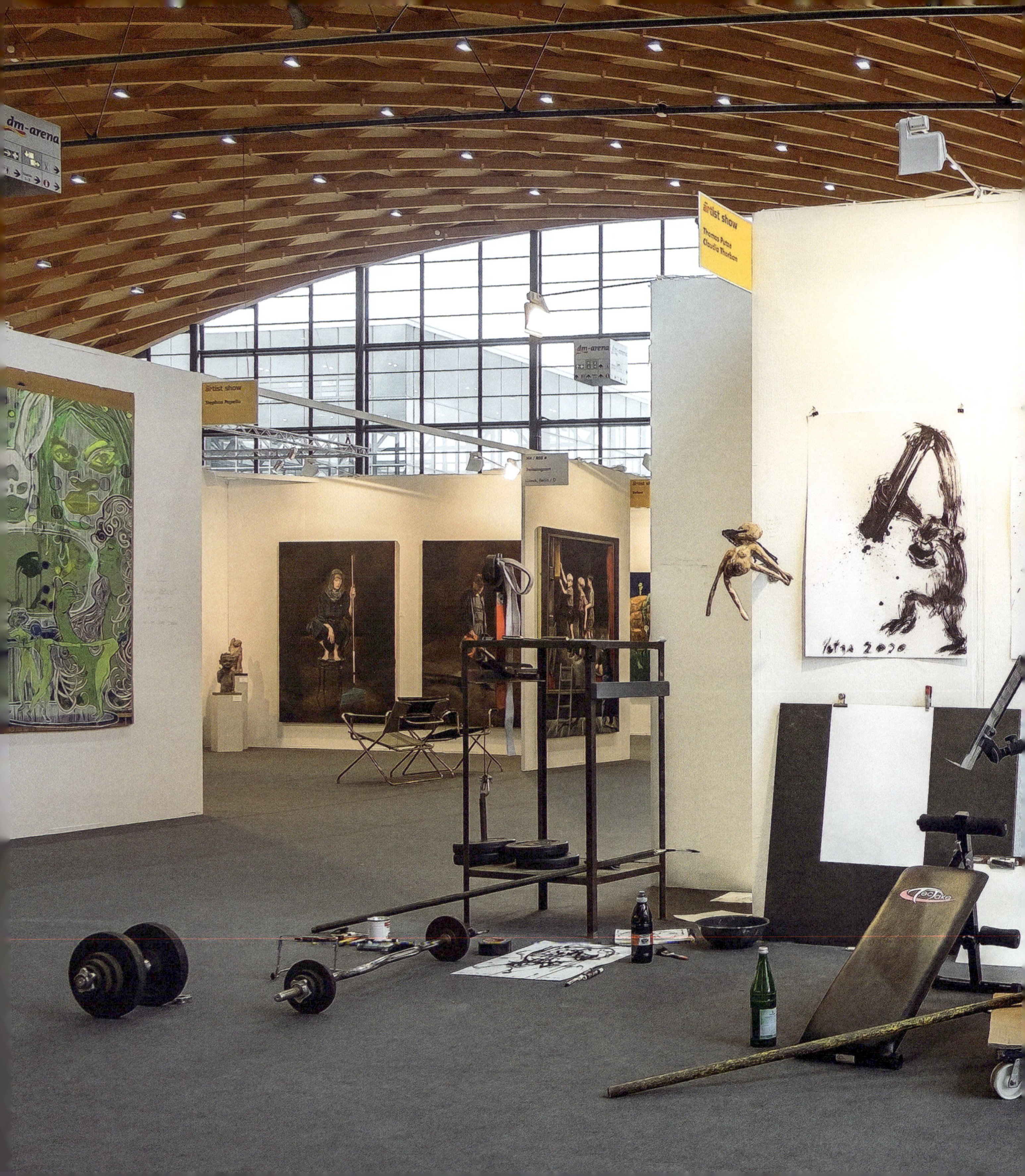
dm-arena
ärtist show
Thomas Putze
Claudia Thorban
dm-arena
ärtist show

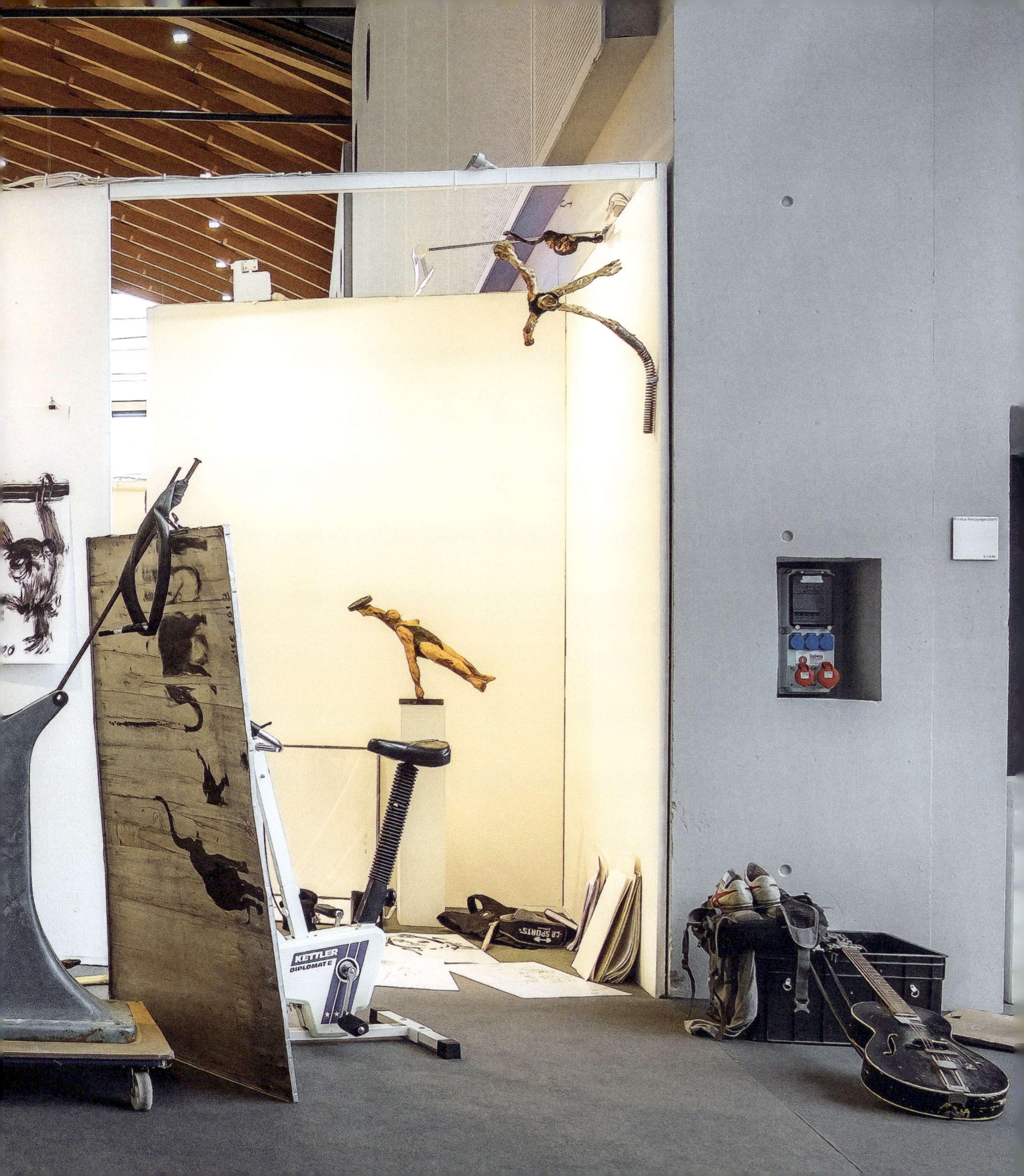
KETTLER
DIPLOMAT E

Februar / February 2020

Kraftakt II

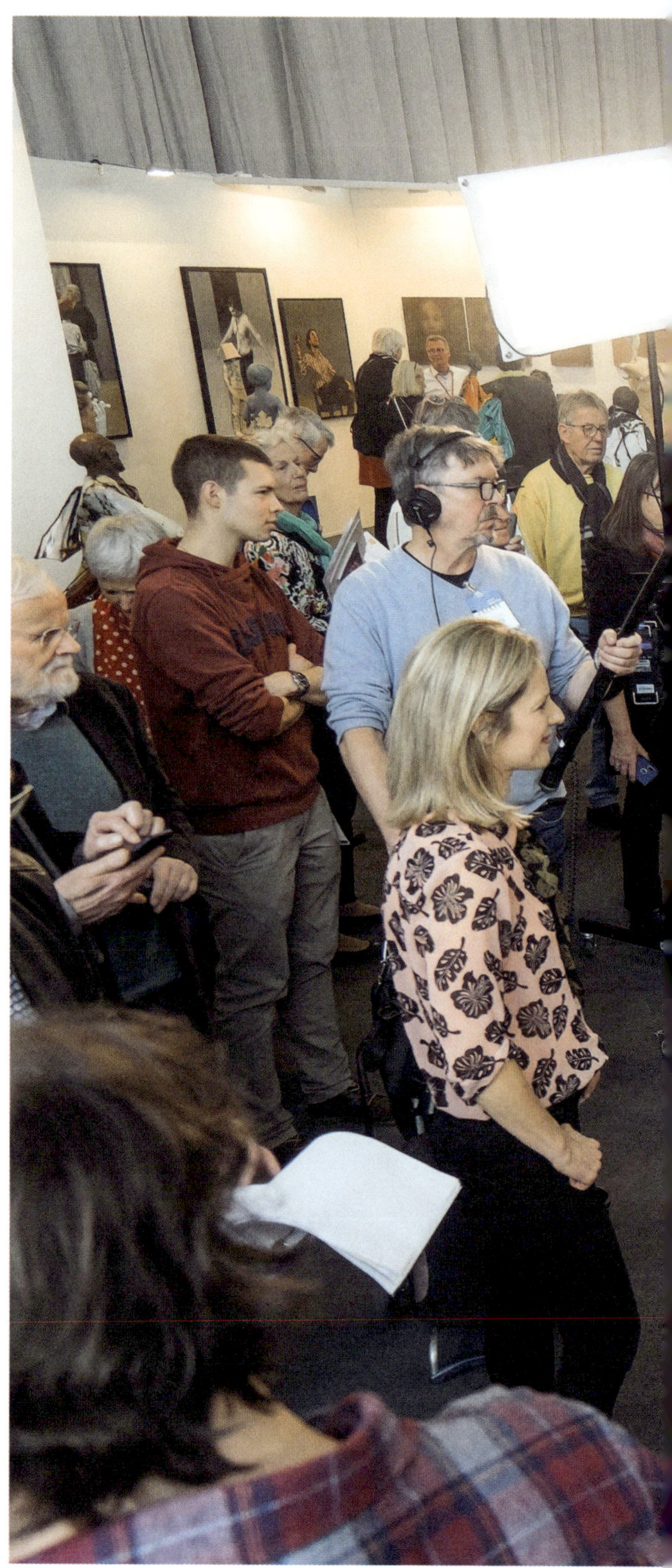

Performance mit selbstgebauten Fitnesszeichenmaschinen. Anlässlich der Art Karlsruhe, 12.–16. Februar 2020, lud Galerist Markus Schacher den Künstler zu einem Kraftakt am Messestand ein: Mit selbstgebauten Fitnessmaschinen zeichnete Thomas Putze unter enormer Kraftanstrengung Porträts der Messebesucher.
Performance with homemade sports equipment. Under enormous physical strain, the artist spent several days portraying visitors to the trade fair using his homemade sports equipment at the stand of Galerie Schacher during Art Karlsruhe, February 12–16, 2020.

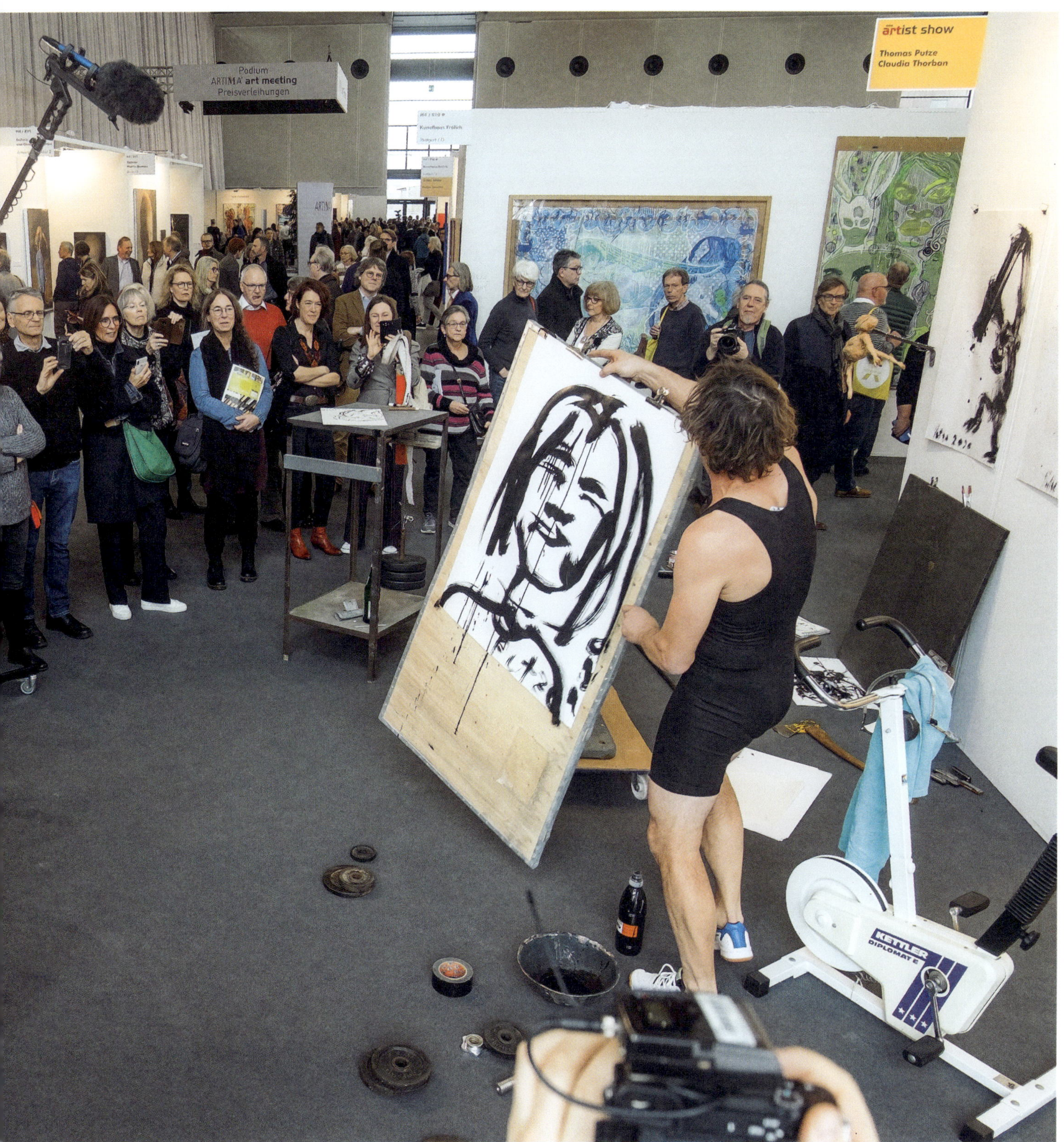
Podium
ARTIMA art meeting
Preisverleihungen
artist show
Thomas Putze
Claudia Thorban
KETTLER
DIPLOMAT E

Mit Biss — 20 Jahre Performance

With Bite— Twenty Years of Performance

Katrin Burtschell

Seit 20 Jahren ist die Performance fester Bestandteil seiner Kunst, trotzdem war es für Thomas Putze zunächst schwierig, sich diese auch als Hauptbestandteil eines Buches vorzustellen. Denn obwohl mit der Performancekunst der eigene Körper, die Fähigkeit des sich Exponierens und die Freude daran im Mittelpunkt stehen, ist es genau das, worauf der Künstler nicht reduziert werden möchte, ist es nicht das, was er intendiert.

Für den vielseitigen Bildhauer, Zeichner und Musiker ist die Performance eine Momentaufnahme, ein Türöffner zum Betrachter und Publikum, ein wohlgeplantes und ausgefeiltes Agieren, das durch spontanes Reagieren auf die Situation eine Veränderung erfährt. Sie ist somit Sinnbild und Ausdruck einer von intuitiver Intelligenz, Instinkt und Wahrnehmung geleiteten Künstlerpersönlichkeit. Vor allem aber ist sie Denken, Zeichnen, Bildhauern und Erfassen mit und durch den Körper. Sie ist die logische Fortsetzung und Erweiterung seines Werkes und macht es dem Künstler möglich, sich selbst und seine Kunst zu ergründen, zu spüren. In dieser Funktion fügt die Performance seinem bildhauerischen und zeichnerischen Werk wichtige Bilder hinzu.

In Thomas Putzes Performances entstehen Einzelbilder, die emblematisch für Aspekte seiner Kunst, seiner eigenen Person, aber auch für eine allgemeine Lebensgültigkeit sind. Bilder, die es dem Betrachter ermöglichen, einen erweiterten Zugang zu seiner Kunst zu finden. Diese Wahrnehmung und Bedeutung hat den Künstler letztendlich überzeugt, seine Performances mit der Publikation *Putze Performances 2000–2020* über den Moment hinaus zu würdigen. Die bewusst getroffene,

Performance has been an integral part of Thomas Putze's art for twenty years; nevertheless it was difficult for him initially to imagine it as the main component of a catalogue. For although his own body, the ability to go out on a limb and the joy in doing so stand at the center of his performance art, this is exactly what the artist does not wish to be reduced to; it is not what he intended. For this multifaceted sculptor, illustrator, and musician, performance is a snapshot of a moment, one that opens the door to observers and audiences, a well-planned and sophisticated act that is then transformed through spontaneous reactions to the situation at hand. It is thus a symbol and expression of an artist personality led by intuitive intelligence, instinct, and perception. Yet above all, it is thinking, drawing, sculpting, and realizing with and through the body. It is the logical continuation and extension of his work, one that makes it possible for the artist to fathom and to sense himself and his art. In this capacity, the performance adds consequential images to his sculptural and illustration work.

In Thomas Putze's performances, individual images are created that are emblematic of aspects of his art, of his own self, but also of a general validity of life—images that enable the viewer to

reduzierte Auswahl aus 20 Jahren Performances bildet den Künstler Thomas Putze, sein Infragestellen und sein Selbstverständnis ab. Sie bildet nicht den Körper Thomas Putze ab. Einen Körper, mit dem der Künstler nach unserem Empfinden nicht schonend umgeht. Aber das ist bei Performances, in der der Körper das Material ist, wohl auch kaum möglich. Performance ist eine spezielle Ausdrucksform, geht an Grenzen, überschreitet diese, hat mit Schmerz, Körperlichkeit, dem über sich selbst und die eigene Schamgrenze Hinauswachsen zu tun. Sie steht irgendwo zwischen Ausdruck, Unterhaltung und Provokation. Provokation im Sinne einer Störung des Gewohnten, einer Unterbrechung. Sie ist aber auch ein Metier, das es zu beherrschen gilt, ein Inszenieren des eigenen Selbst, eines Momentes und Augenblicks. Dies zu tun ohne gängige Klischees zu bedienen, ist es, was Putzes Performances ausmacht.
Juni 2014, als Baum getarnt, die Füße in Baumwurzeln steckend, überhängt mit Ästen und Zweigen, mit Plastiktüten und Taschen voller Grünzeug, marschiert Thomas Putze von seinem Atelier in den Wagenhallen zum Hauptbahnhof Stuttgart, um dort die

gain amplified access to his art. Such perception and meaning ultimately convinced the artist to recognize his performances over and above the moment with this catalogue, *Putze Performances 2000–2020*. The deliberate, reduced selection from twenty years of performances represents the artist Thomas Putze, his inquiring mind, and his self-image. It does not represent his body—a body that, in our opinion, the artist does not go easy on; in any case, in performance, where the body is the material, that is nigh-on impossible. Performance is a special form of expression; it pushes boundaries, oversteps them, is about pain, corporeality, about reaching beyond oneself and one's own inhibitions. It lies somewhere between expression, entertainment, and provocation—provocation in the sense of a disturbance of what is usual, an interruption. But it is also a métier that one needs to be in control of, a staging of one's own self, of a moment, an instance. To do this without resorting to established clichés is what constitutes Putze's performances.
In June 2014, camouflaged as a tree, with his feet pushed into tree roots, overhanging with boughs and branches, with bags and plastic sacks full of green waste, Thomas Putze tramped from his studio at the Wagenhallen to

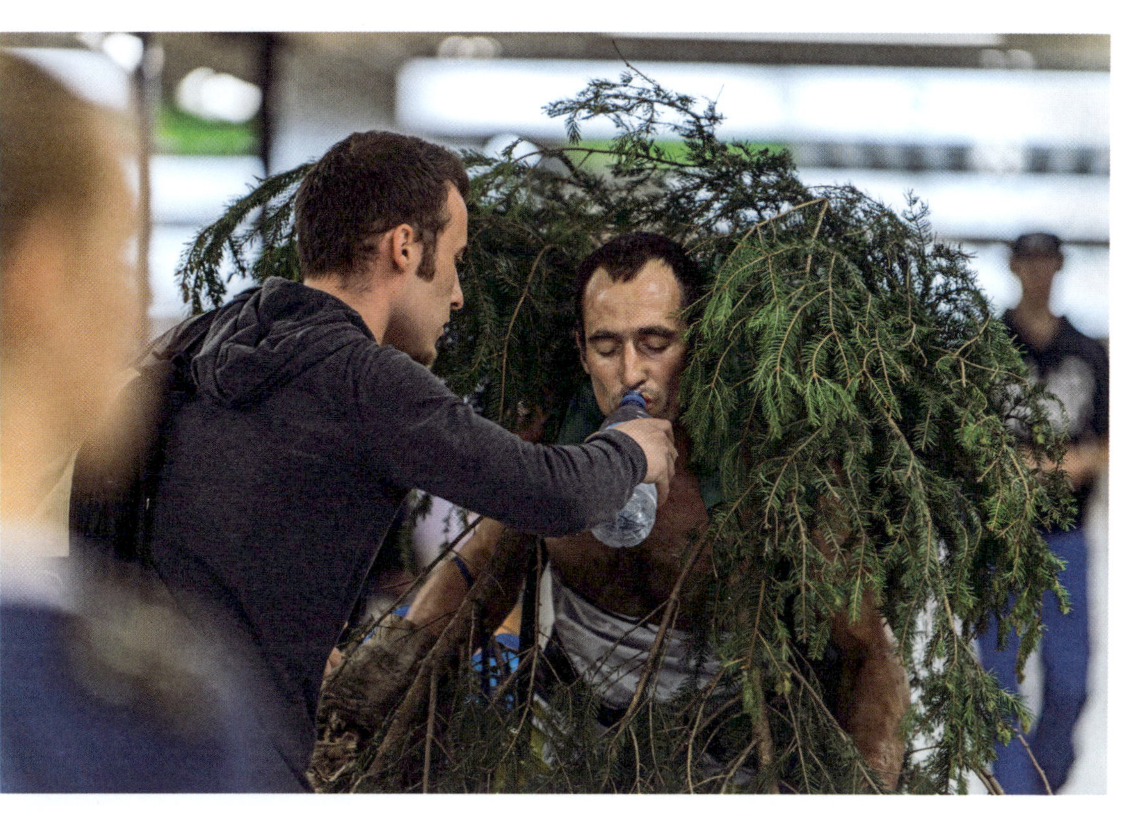

Passage, 2014, Ausstellungsprojekt / exhibition project *Transition #2*, Klettpassage, Hauptbahnhof / Main Station, Stuttgart

Einkaufspassage zu durchqueren (S.100/101). Vorbei an irritierten Passanten, die dem Künstler mangelnde Zurechnungsfähigkeit attestieren, an Fahrgästen, die kaum Notiz davon nehmen und zu ihrer Bahn eilen. Andere bleiben stehen und verfolgen das Geschehen, ein junger Mann gibt dem schwitzenden

Stuttgart Main Station and crisscrossed the Klettpassage shopping arcade—passing confounded bystanders who would swear the artist had lost his mind, passing passengers who barely noticed him as they rushed for their train (pp.100/101). Others, including a young man offering a drink to the artist, who was sweating and groaning under his

und unter seiner Last und dem unbequemen Schuhwerk ächzendem Künstler zu trinken.
Juli 2016, Thomas Putze überquert als flügge werdender *Ästling*, sinnbildlich für den die Akademie verlassenden Kunststudenten, das Areal der Freien Kunstakademie Nürtingen (S. 94–97). In Luftpolsterfolie gewickelt und ausschließlich durch diese gesichert, verfolgt er die Absicht, sich von Baum zu Baum fortzubewegen. Die Zuschauer halten phasenweise die Luft an. Als der Künstler vor Erschöpfung kaum mehr kletterfähig ist, unterstützen sie ihn. Es entstehen Situationen wie in mittelalterlichen Darstellungen der

load and his uncomfortable footwear, stood there following the goings-on.
In July 2016, Thomas Putze traversed the grounds of the Freie Kunstakademie Nürtingen (Independent Academy of Fine Arts) as an almost fully fledged nestling, a symbol of the art students that were leaving the academy (pp. 94–97). Swathed in bubble wrap and safeguarded only by this, his intention was to move from tree to tree. Viewers on occasion held their breath and lent support when the artist was barely able to climb from exhaustion. Scenes played out like medieval depictions of the Deposition of the Cross. The viewer became a part of this tableau vivant,

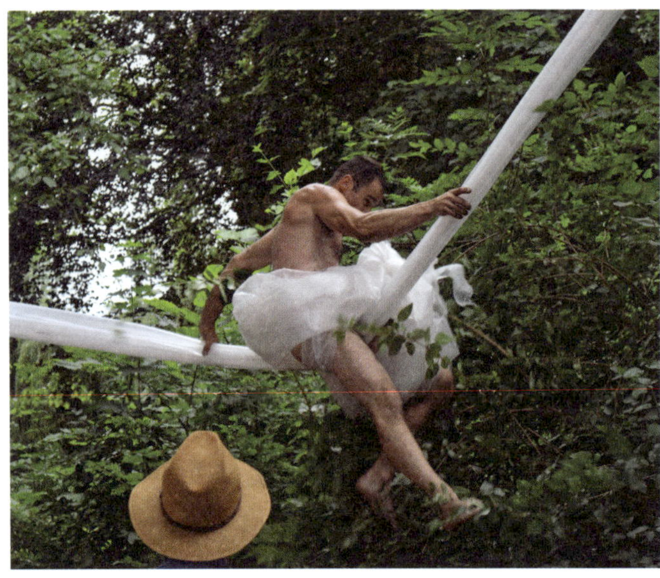

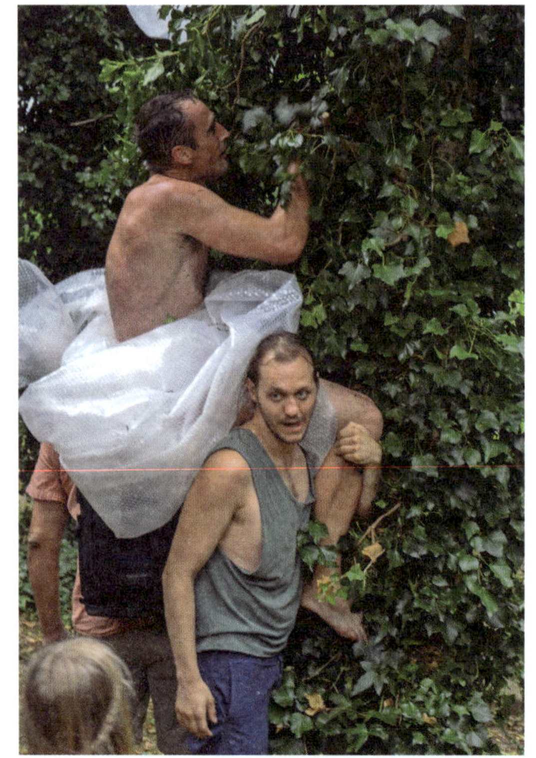

Ästling (Nestling), 2016, Freie Kunstakademie Nürtingen (FKN)

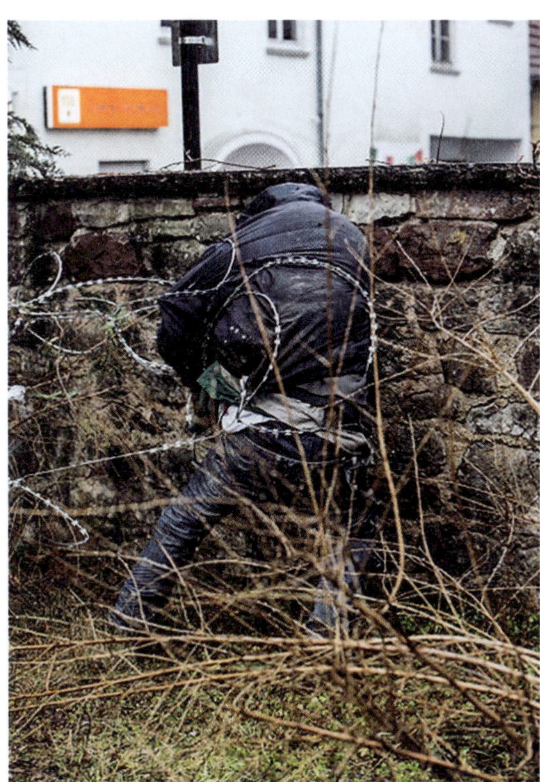

Das Schloss (The Castle), 2018, Galerie Schlichtenmaier, Schloss Dätzingen

Kreuzabnahme. Der Zuschauer wird Teil dieses Tableau vivant, wird zu Assistenzfigur eines lebendigen Bildes. Januar 2018, ein eisiger, verregneter Vormittag im Schlosspark von Schloss Dätzingen. Thomas Putze performt zur Finissage seiner Ausstellung *Mitspieler* in der Galerie Schlichtenmaier (S. 16/17). Der Künstler muss sich den Zugang zu seiner Ausstellung erarbeiten, nachdem er ihn sich selbst zuvor verbaut hat: er klettert über einen Sperrspitzenzaun, der das Schloss umgibt, kämpft sich dann durch den selbst installierten Natodraht, mehr oder weniger geschützt durch dicke Kleiderschichten. Phasenweise hängt er komplett fest, hören wir Zuschauer nur das Geräusch des zerreißenden Stoffes. Er bleibt liegen, die Zuschauer wollen ihn aus der misslichen Lage, in die er sich gebracht hat, befreien, hoffen insgeheim, dass er aufgibt, was er natürlich nicht tut. Eine

became the supporting figure of a living picture.
January 2018, an icy, rainy morning in the gardens of Schloss Dätzingen (pp. 16/17): Thomas Putze was performing there for the final day of his exhibition *Mitspieler* (Teammate) at Galerie Schlichtenmaier. After first obstructing the exhibition himself, the artist had to then work out how to access it: he climbed over an iron gate topped with spearhead finials that surrounds the stately home and, to a greater or lesser extent protected with thick layers of clothing, fought his way through a razor-barbed-wire he had installed himself. At times, he hung there completely unable to move; we, the viewer, would only hear the sounds of ripping fabric. He just lay there. The onlookers wanted to free him from the predicament that he had gotten into but secretly hoped that he would give up—which of course he did not do. A tensile test for him and the viewer to the point of being excruciating,

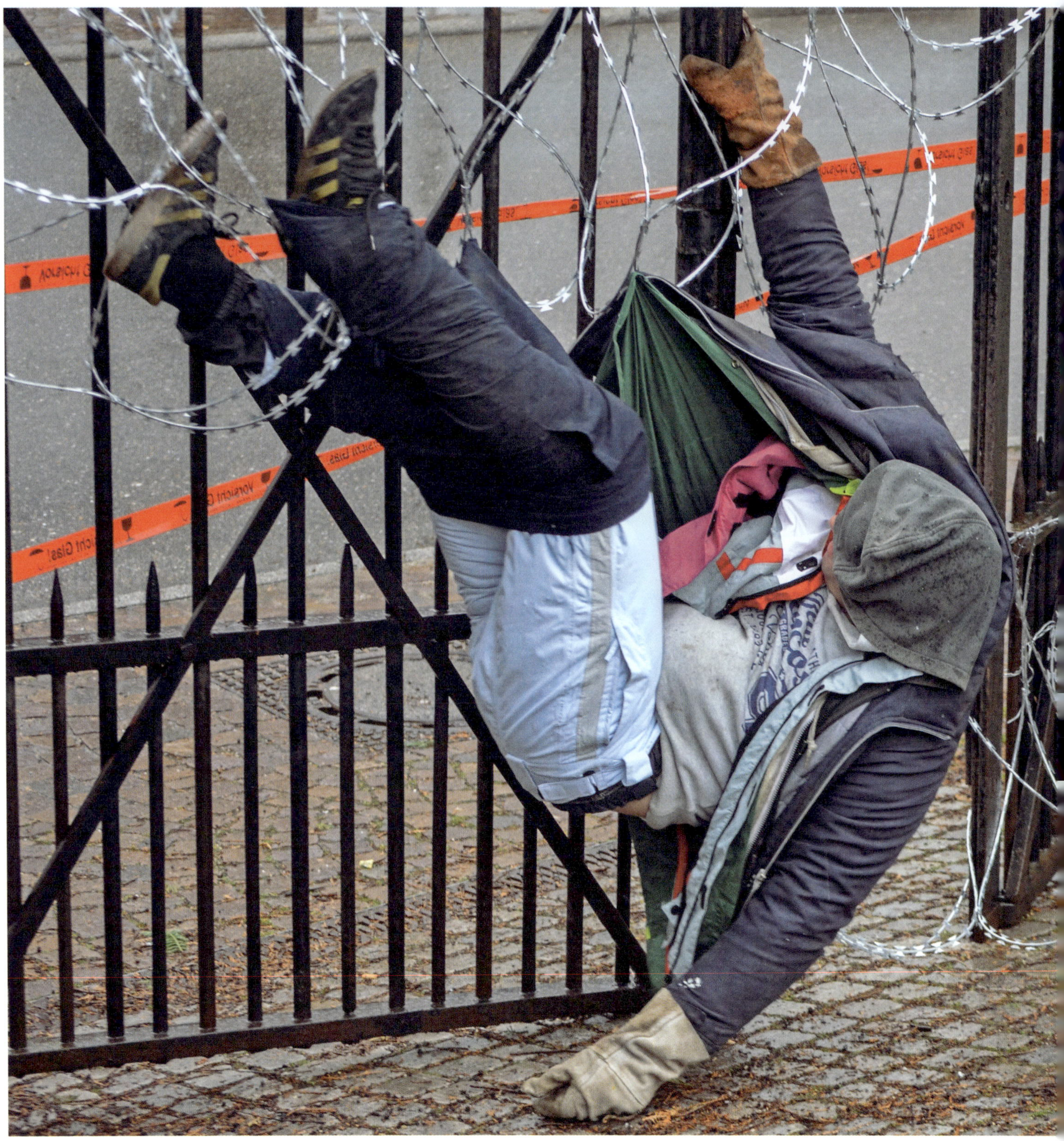

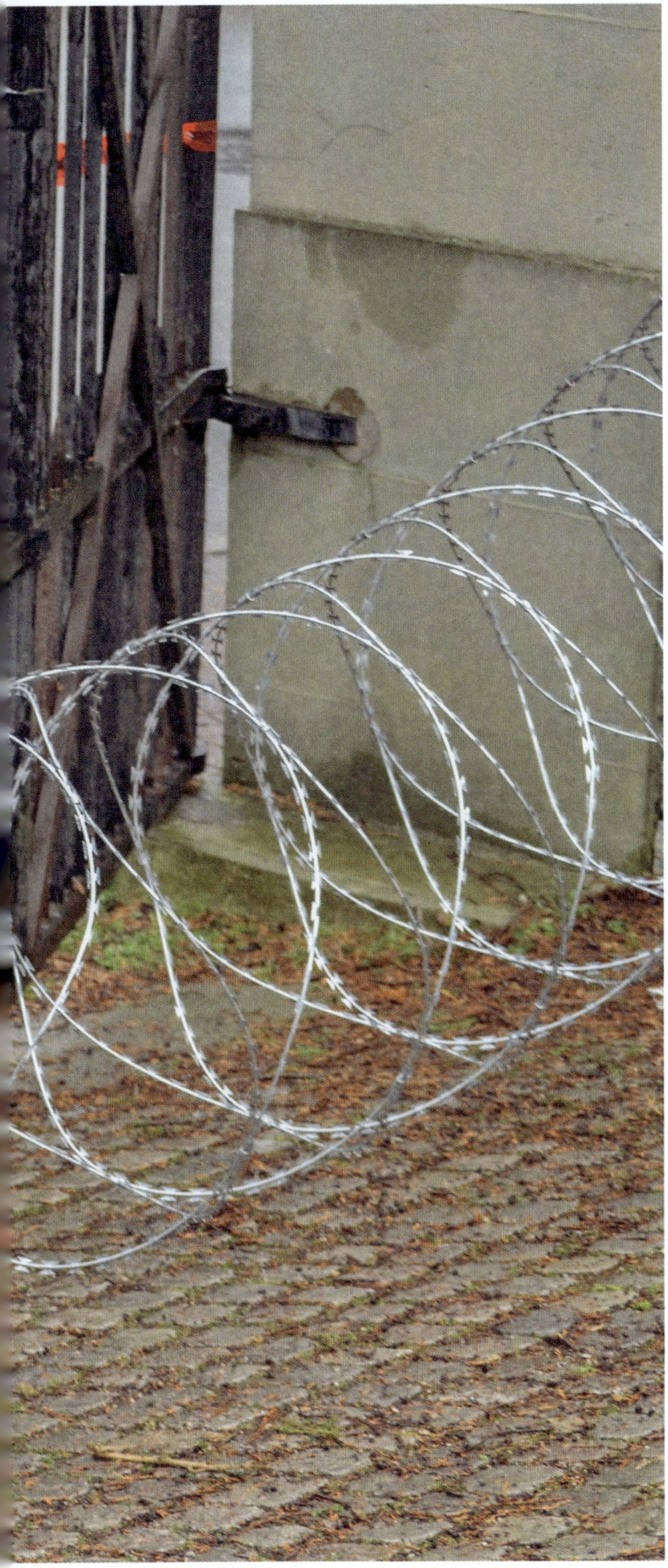

Januar / January 2018

Das Schloss

Performance mit Natodraht und Kleidung. Zur Finissage der Ausstellung *Mitspieler* am 20. Januar 2018 in der Galerie Schlichtenmaier Schloss Dätzingen kämpfte sich der Künstler, zu seinem Schutz in mehrere Lagen Kleidung gehüllt, durch eine Installation aus Natodraht. Ausgangspunkt der Performance war Kafkas Roman *Das Schloss*.
Performance with razor-barbed wire and clothing. For the closing day of the exhibition *Mitspieler* (Teammate), on January 20, 2018, at Galerie Schlichtmaier Schloss Dätzingen, the artist, protected by several layers of clothing, fought his way through an installation of razor-barbed wire. The inspiration for the performance was Kafka's novel *Das Schloss* (The Castle).

Zerreißprobe für ihn und die Betrachter bis zur Unerträglichkeit, die er am Schluss durch ein humorvolles Ende auflöst.
Den Plan plötzlich ändern: ja, aber aufgeben: nein, Scheitern ist erwünscht. Der Bildhauer geht in seinen Performances genauso wie bei seinen Skulpturen an die Grenze dessen, was möglich ist, bis es bricht, nicht mehr funktioniert, an die Grenzen seiner eigenen, zugegebenermaßen gewaltigen Kraft. So dass man als Zuschauer oft das Bedürfnis hat einzugreifen. Putzes Performances leben vom „Verspielen" und davon, dieses Verspielen durch den nächsten Schritt in etwas Richtiges umzuwandeln. Auf diese Weise baut er auch seine Skulpturen. Er selbst beschreibt diesen Prozess und das Resultat daraus als „Vernarbungen von Verletzungen" oder als „zu erhellenden Formen ausgewachsene formale Fehler."
Der ehemals gelernte Baumpfleger und leidenschaftliche Kletterer weiß, was er tut, kalkuliert das Risiko und wenn es für uns schon halsbrecherisch aussieht, bewegt er sich sicheren Griffs weiter fort. Es sind waghalsige Klettertouren durch die eigene Kunst, durch Natur, Glaube, Menschsein und vor allem durch das Künstlersein. Dabei kreiert Putze in seinen Performances

which he ultimately resolved with a humorous ending.
Change the plan? Sure. But give up? No. Failure is welcomed. The sculptor pushes the boundaries of what is possible, both in his performances and in his sculptures, until it ruptures, no longer functions; he pushes the limits of his own—admittedly tremendous—fortitude. So much so that you, as the observer, often feel the need to intervene. Putze's performances live from "the risk of losing" and transform this risk by making the next step one into something proper. And this is how he constructs his sculptures too. He describes this process and what results from it as "forming healing scars" or as "bringing light to full-blown formal transgressions."
The former trained arborist and passionate climber knows exactly what he is doing; he calculates the risk and, just when it appears breakneck, continues onwards with a firm grip. These are daring climbing routes through his own art, through nature, belief, being human, and above all through being an artist. At the same time, Putze invariably creates a wholly individual aesthetic during his performances. He is often surrounded by a well-organized chaos created from the waste of civilization, meters of white cloth, nakedness, dirt, nature, mismatched pieces from his studio,

immer wieder eine ganz eigene Ästhetik. Oft umgibt ihn ein wohlorganisiertes Chaos aus Zivilisationsmüll, meterlangen weißen Tüchern, Nacktheit, Schmutz, Natur, Versatzstücken des eigenen Ateliers, Werkzeug, Material. Das Einswerden mit dem Material und der Umgebung spielt eine maßgebliche Rolle. Wo Putze auftaucht, macht er den Ort zum Atelier – und wer schon mal sein Atelier, ein Sammelsurium aus Arbeitsmaterialien, Fundstücken, vollendeten Skulpturen und bearbeiteten Objekten, besucht hat, weiß, was das heißt. Nirgendwo wurde dies augenfälliger, als in der cleanen, kühlen Ästhetik der Messehalle der Art Karlsruhe im Februar 2020, bei seiner Performance *Kraftakt II* (S. 8/9). Hier störte er

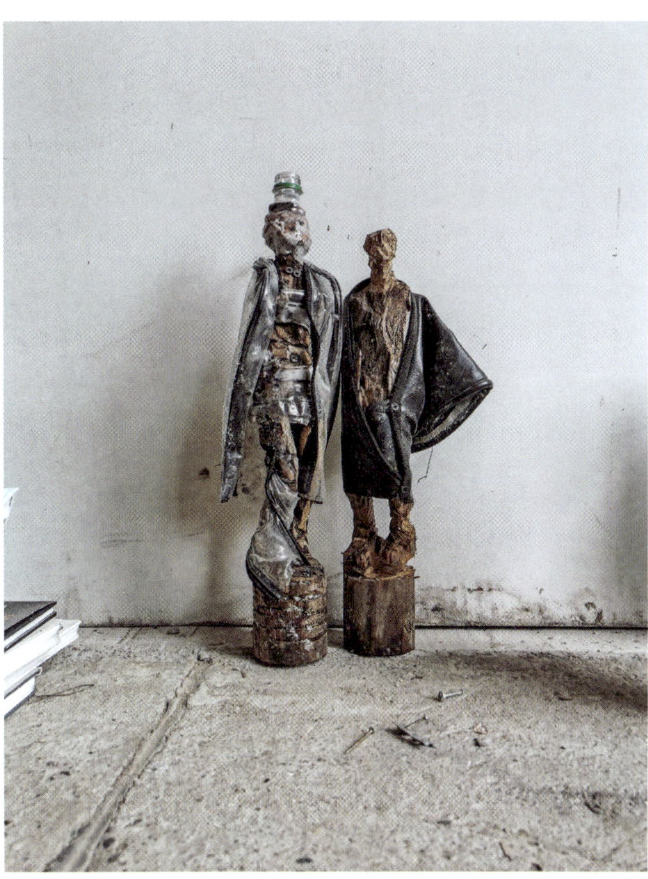

Überlebende (Survivors), 2012–2020, Holz und Kunststoff / wood and plastic, je / each ca. 45 x 12 x 20 cm

tools, materials. Becoming one with the materials and the environment plays a crucial role. Wherever he appears, Putze transforms the site into his studio, and those who have visited his—a mélange of work materials, found objects, completed sculptures, and objects in the making—knows what this means. Nowhere was this more noticeable than in the clean, cool aesthetic of the trade fair Art Karlsruhe in February 2020 with his performance *Kraftakt II* (Act of Strength II, pp. 8/9). Here he not only disturbs the aesthetic sensibilities of many a visitor but at the end also pays little mind to the trade fair's regulations, thus posing key questions to the art industry and to us: Does art have to be elite and unapproachable? If it has to conform, doesn't it then stop being art? Does it not belong to the people, is it not part of the people? Important questions with which the leading art historian Jerry Saltz grapples constantly by calling for art to be brought out from its ivory tower.

For Putze, performance is something self-evident, something primordial, and he draws a basic principle of his performance art from his theological training. His teacher Fritz Gaiser provided him with the impetus: "It's no good standing up for something; you have to put yourself out there." Another important impulse on the path to performance was his occupation with Joseph Beuys during his studies. Putze became aware that it wasn't enough to reach or shock the viewer by simply hanging a beautiful picture on the wall. Rather, sometimes

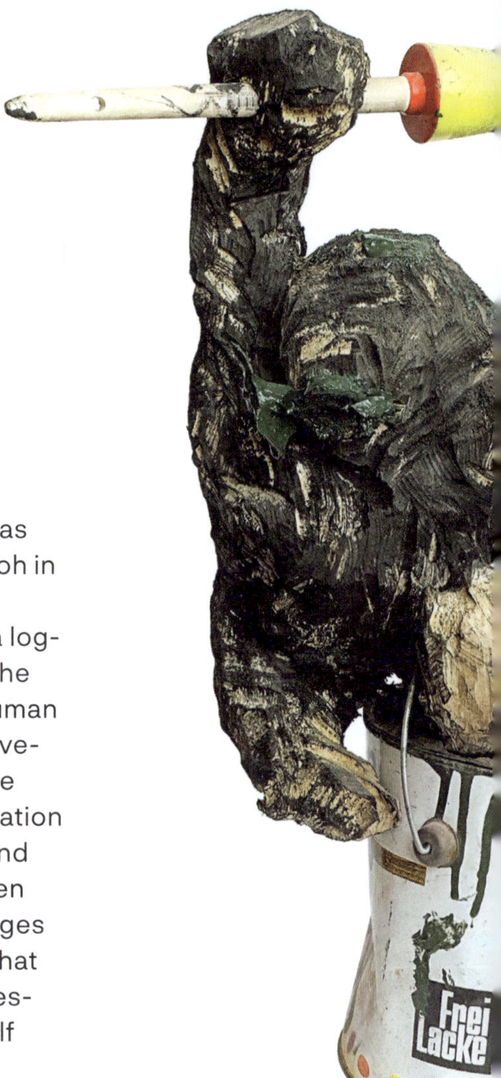

nicht nur das ästhetische Empfinden manches Besuchers, sondern scherte sich am Ende auch reichlich wenig um die Messevorschriften und stellte dadurch wichtige Fragen an den Kunstbetrieb und an uns: muss Kunst elitär und unnahbar sein? Muss sie konform gehen, hört sie dann nicht auf, Kunst zu sein? Gehört sie nicht dem Menschen, zum Menschen dazu? Eine wichtige Frage, mit der sich auch der amerikanische Kunsthistoriker Jerry Saltz unablässig auseinandersetzt und fordert, die Kunst aus ihrem Elfenbeinturm herauszuholen.
Für Putze ist die Performance etwas Selbstverständliches, etwas ganz Urmenschliches, und eine Grundlage für seine Performancekunst liegt in seinem theologischen Studium begründet. Sein Lehrer Fritz Gaiser gab ihm den Impuls mit: „Es bringt nichts, sich für etwas einzusetzen, man muss sich aussetzen". Ein weiterer wichtiger Impulsgeber auf dem Weg zu Performance war die Beschäftigung

you have to put yourself on display as the exhibit, as happened in Gütersloh in March 2019 (pp. 82–85).
Putze's performance art is for him a logical consequence to the questions he asks himself as an artist and as a human being, and to his tendency to positively flourish in front of an audience. He draws his energy from the confrontation with people, with those opposite, and finds it "a favorable experience when moments such as those at vernissages can lead to an intense presence—that is, produce a stronger audience presence—which usually manifests itself during a strong performance.
Even when the performer knows exactly what he's doing and approaches it with the utmost professionalism, aplomb, and self-confidence, only in retrospect does he sometimes become aware of his nakedness and exposure and in hindsight is mortified. Children as well as adults well versed In art are astounded in equal measure when they watch him perform. While children ask unabashed questions

mit Joseph Beuys während des Kunststudiums. Putze wurde bewusst, dass es nicht reicht, einfach nur ein schönes Bild an die Wand zu hängen, um den Betrachter zu erreichen oder zu erschüttern. Sondern, dass man manchmal schon auch sich selbst als Exponat ausstellen muss, so geschehen in Gütersloh im März 2019 (S. 82–85). Putzes Performancekunst ist für ihn eine logische Konsequenz aus den Fragen, die er an sich als Künstler und als Menschen stellt, und aus seiner Veranlagung, vor Publikum förmlich aufzublühen. Er zieht seine Energie aus der Konfrontation mit Menschen, mit dem Gegenüber und empfindet es als „ein beglückendes Erlebnis, wenn man Augenblicke, etwa wie bei einer Vernissage, zu einer intensiven Gegenwart führen kann, also eine stärkere Präsenz des Publikums herstellen kann, die sich in der Regel bei einer starken Performance einstellt."

Auch wenn der Performer genau weiß, was er tut, und mit der größtmöglichen Professionalität, Souveränität und Selbstbewusstsein an die Sache herangeht, passiert es manchmal, dass er sich erst in der Rückschau seiner Nacktheit und Ausgesetztheit bewusst wird und sich im Nachhinein schämt. Kinder wie kunstversierte Erwachsene staunen gleichermaßen, wenn sie ihn beim Performen beobachten. Während Kinder die ungenierte Fragen stellen, was macht der da und warum, neigen die Erwachsenen dazu, kategorische Antworten zu haben, stellen sich aber

about what he's doing and why, the adults tend to have categorical answers, but deep inside they are also asking the same question: Why is he doing that? Why is he standing naked in the empty recess on the exterior facade of a Gothic cathedral (pp. 38–41), why is he sitting like a cheeky beaver in the unsteady canopy of a tree, sawing and clamoring, climbing and swimming to his own beaver's lodge (pp. 78–81), an installation created for the Donaugalerie in the summer of 2019? Why is he smearing himself with eggnog, mud, earth, and travertine dust and bellowing stark naked in the faces of the surprised exhibition visitors, or swinging against a giant metal sign as a naked human pendulum (pp. 90/91)? Those who are now reminded of Wolfgang Flatz's performance *Demontage IX* in Tiflis in 1991, where he swung like a human bell-clapper between two sheets of steel until he lost consciousness from the impact, are on the wrong track here. It is not Putze's intention to push his pain threshold, or to explore the limits of his body's own resilience and the onlookers' nerves in an almost masochistic and exhibitionist manner, even if it might come to that on occasion.

Instead, Putze neutralizes such moments time and again with his omnipresent humor, a certain self-irony in all seriousness, and most of all through dialogue with the viewers. It is the delight in the balancing act while all eyes are upon him and the faith that the mutual fraught attentiveness will turn into a small service of worship in which everyone is recharged emotionally or

Panscher (Thrashing and Splashing)
aus der Serie / from the series *Tachisten* (Tachists), 2013–2016,
Pappel, Tusche, Mixed Media / poplar, ink, mixed media, 48 x 40 x 30 cm

tief im Inneren dieselbe Frage, warum macht er das? Warum stellt er sich nackt in die leere Statuennische an der Außenfassade einer gotischen Kathedrale (S. 38–41), warum sitzt er als frecher Biber im wackeligen Wipfel eines Baumes, sägt und tobt, klettert und schwimmt zu seinem eigenen Biberbau (S. 78–81), einer Installation, die anlässlich der Donaugalerie im Sommer 2019 entstanden ist? Warum schmiert er sich voll mit Eierlikör, Schlamm, Erde, Travertinstaub, brüllt splitterfasernackt den überraschten Ausstellungsbesuchern ins Gesicht oder schwingt als nacktes menschliches Pendel gegen eine riesiges Blechschild (S. 90/91)?

Wer sich hierbei nun an Wolfgang Flatz' Performance *Demontage IX* in Tiflis 1991 erinnert fühlt, bei der er als menschlicher Glockenknöppel zwischen zwei Stahlwänden schwang, bis er durch den Aufprall das Bewusstsein verlor, erinnert fühlt, ist auf dem Holzweg. Putzes Intention ist es nicht, bis an die Schmerzgrenze zu gehen, oder in fast schon masochistischer und auch exhibitionistischer Art und Weise die Grenzen der Belastbarkeit des eigenen Körpers und der Nerven des Zuschauers auszuloten, auch wenn es hier und da zu solchen Momenten kommen mag.

theologically that pushes him and allows him to cross the threshold of shame while performing.

Probably the most emblematic and challenging performance of his career regarding this was in November 2019, for the exhibition *Affentheater* (Monkey Theater, pp. 88/89) in Rottweil. Already during the opening speech, the artist was crouching in a high-up window recess and started to behave in an apish manner. He climbed riotously down into the surprised crowd of onlookers and began mixing among the audience, insulting them as he went while slipping into a suit and sneakers; he was then served a sparkling wine and was suddenly one of the crowd looking at his own work. As a symbol of an artist standing on the margins of society and ultimately taking part in the circus, you will not find a stronger one.

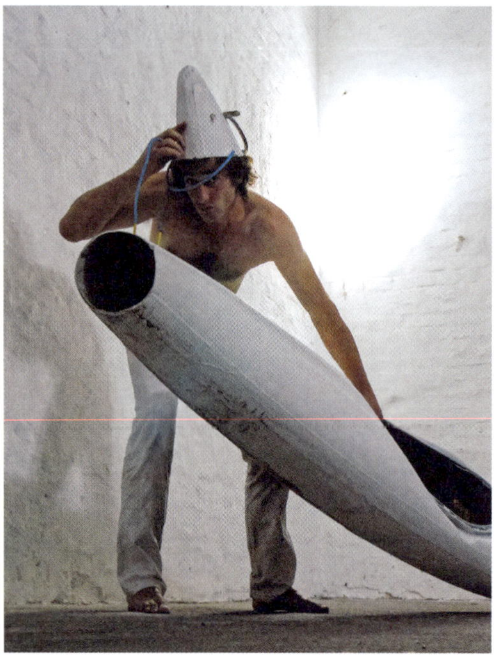

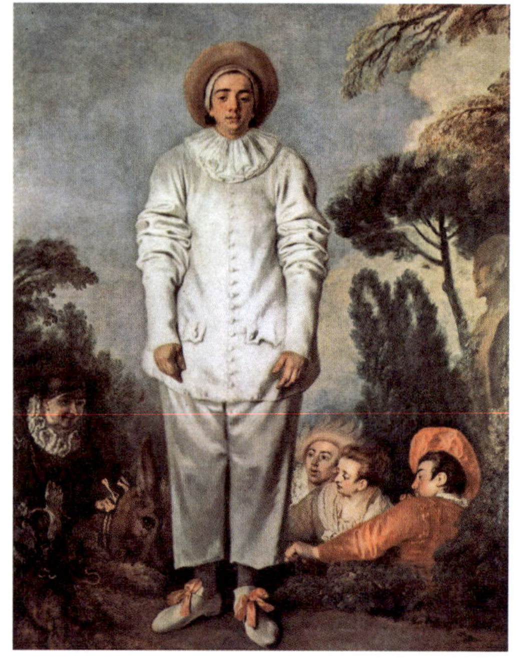

Thomas Putze. Oben ohne (Topless), September 2011, Städtische Galerie Delmenhorst
Jean-Antoine Watteau, *Pierrot*, 1718–1719, Öl auf Leinwand / oil on canvas, 184,5 x 149,5 cm, Louvre Paris

Diese Momente entwaffnet Putze aber immer wieder durch seinen über allem schwebenden Humor, einer gewissen Selbstironie bei aller Ernsthaftigkeit und vor allem durch den Dialog mit den Zuschauern. Die Lust an dem Balanceakt vor aller Augen und das Vertrauen darauf, dass die gemeinsame gespannte Aufmerksamkeit zu einem kleinen Gottesdienst wird, bei dem jeder auftankt, in seelischer oder geistiger Hinsicht, sind es, die ihn antreiben und ihn, während er performt, die eigene Schamgrenze überschreiten lassen.
Die diesbezüglich wohl emblematischste und herausforderndste Performance seiner Karriere, war die im November 2019, anlässlich der Ausstellung *Affentheater* in Rottweil (S. 88/89). Bereits während der Eröffnungsrede kauerte der nackte Künstler in einer hoch gelegenen Fensternische und begann sich äffisch zu verhalten.
Er kletterte tobend nach unten in die überraschte Zuschauermenge und begann, Beschimpfungen ausstoßend, sich unters Publikum zu mischen, während er in Anzug und Turnschuhe schlüpfte, sich einen Sekt reichen ließ und plötzlich einer von allen war, sein eigenes Werk betrachtend. Ein stärkeres Sinnbild dafür, wie es ist, als Künstler am Rande der Gesellschaft zu stehen und am Ende den Zirkus doch mitzumachen, kann man kaum finden.
Hier drängt sich ein kunsthistorischer Vergleich zum Thema des Künstlers als Außenseiter der Gesellschaft auf, zu Antoine Watteaus Gemälde *Pierrot* aus dem Jahr 1718. Da steht ein Clown erstarrt im Bildvordergrund in seinem Kostüm. Die Figuren im Hintergrund haben den Blick von ihm abgewandt und betrachten einen Esel. Dieses Gemälde Watteaus wurde oft als Selbstporträt des Künstlers als trauriger Clown interpretiert. Eine ambivalente Erscheinung, schwankend zwischen seiner Rolle als Unterhalter und seinem Dasein als Randständiger in der Gesellschaft, was der Künstler ja auch ist.
Putze empfindet diesen Zustand tatsächlich oft, sein Werk dreht sich um das sich Infragestellen und Reflektieren der Rolle des Künstlers in der Gesellschaft. Davon erzählen auch seine Skulpturen und Zeichnungen, oft begegnen uns darin vom Leben gebeutelte Kreaturen. Aber ganz anders als Watteaus trauriger Clown recken sie die Faust die Höhe, ergeben sie sich nicht ihrem Schicksal, weigern sie sich, Opfer zu sein. Künstler und Werk haben den nötigen Witz und Biss, nicht unterzugehen. Bleibt zu hoffen, dass wir noch mehr Putze zu sehen bekommen in der Zukunft.

An art historical comparison suggests the pathos of the artist as a social outsider, or Antoine Watteau's painting *Pierrot*, from 1718, in which a clown stands frozen in the foreground in his Pierrot outfit. The figures in the background have turned their gazes away from him and instead are looking at a donkey. The painting by Watteau was often interpreted as a self-portrait of the artist as a sad clown. An ambivalent image, fluctuating between his role as an entertainer and his existence as a marginalized figure in society, which indeed the artist also is.
Putze often feels this way, in fact; his work revolves around questioning and reflecting on the social role of the artist. His sculptures and drawings—in which we frequently encounter creations shaken by life—tell of this too. But in contrast to Watteau's sad clown, they raise their fists upwards, do not surrender to their fate, refuse to be victims. Artist and work have the wit and bite necessary in order not to founder. We remain hopeful that we will get to see somewhat more of Putze in the future.

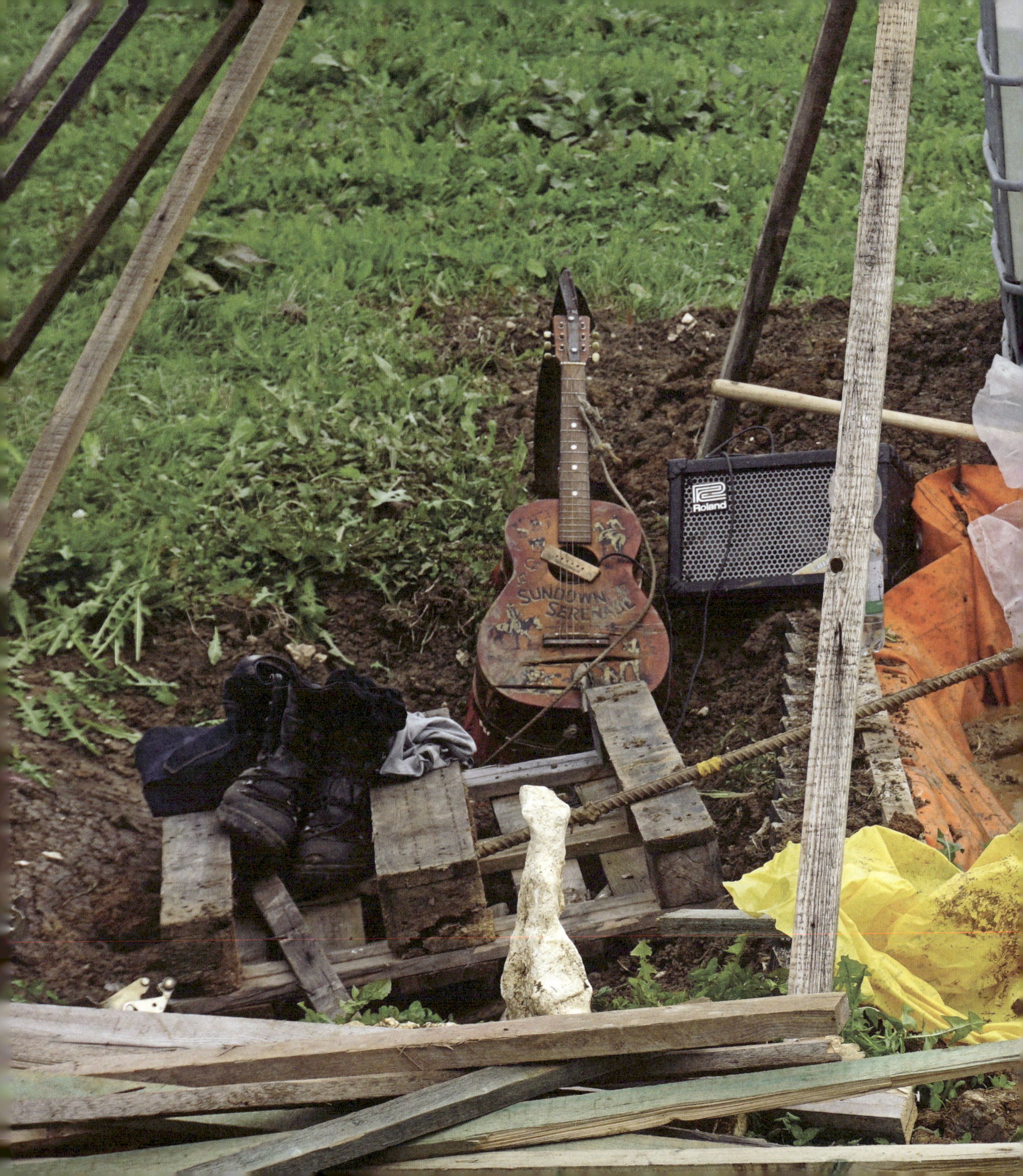
Roland
SUNDOWN SERENADE

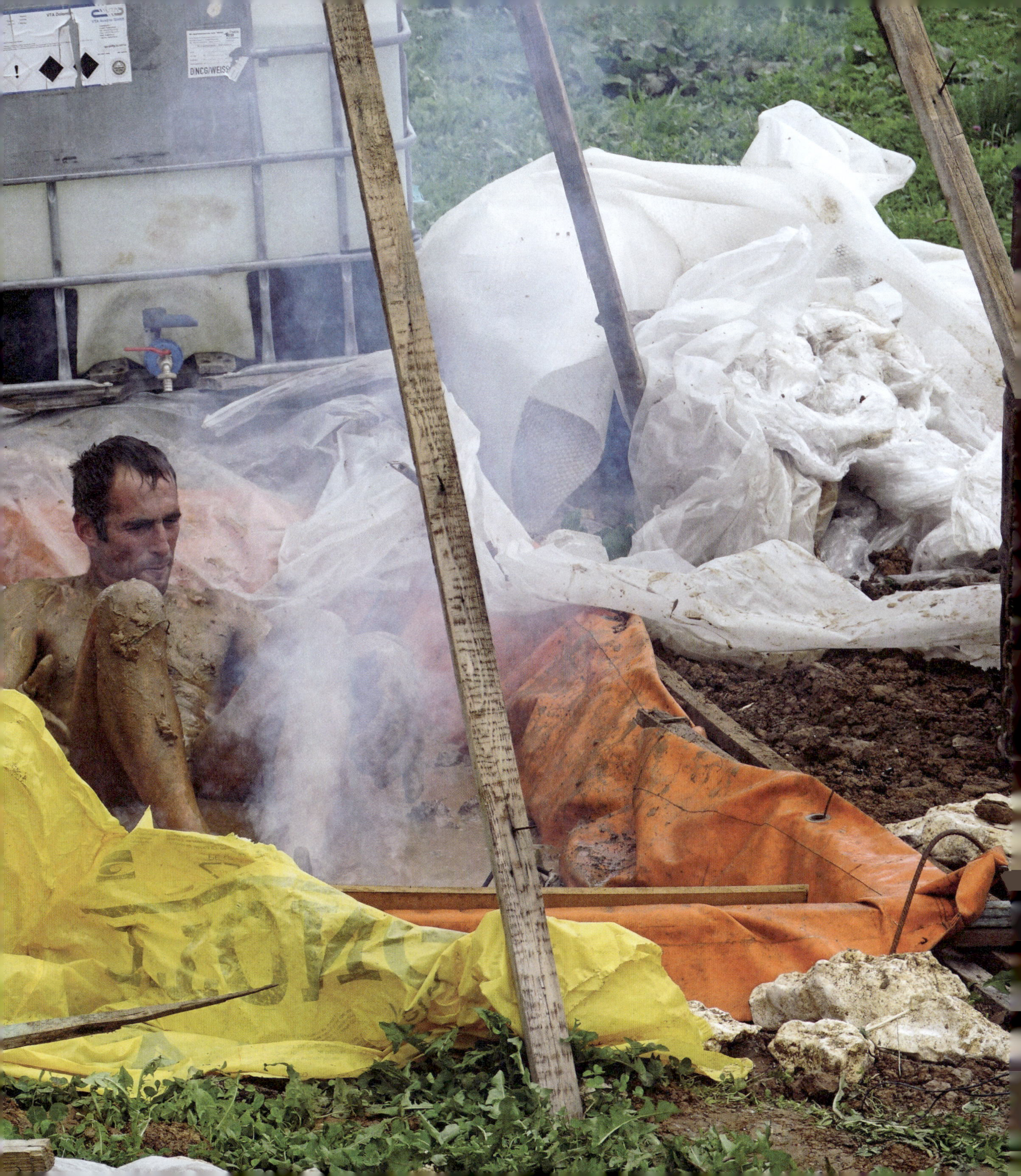
DNCG/WEIS

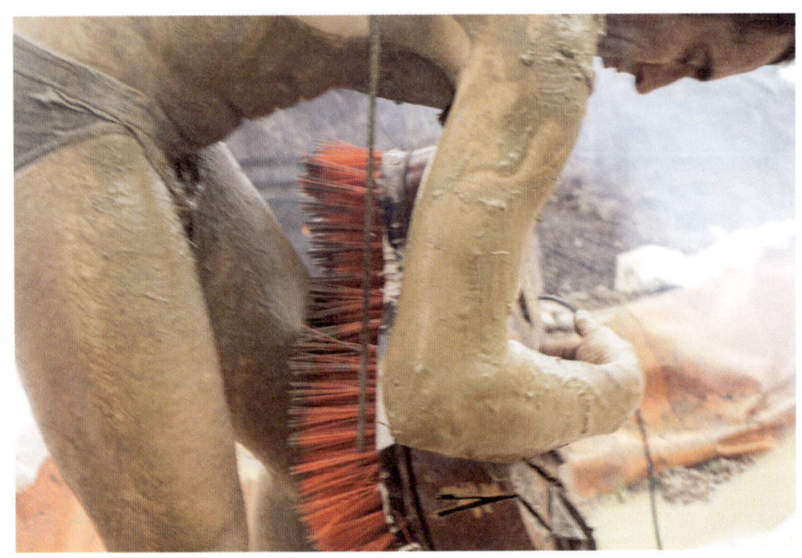

Sommer /
Summer
2017

Heiden-
spaß

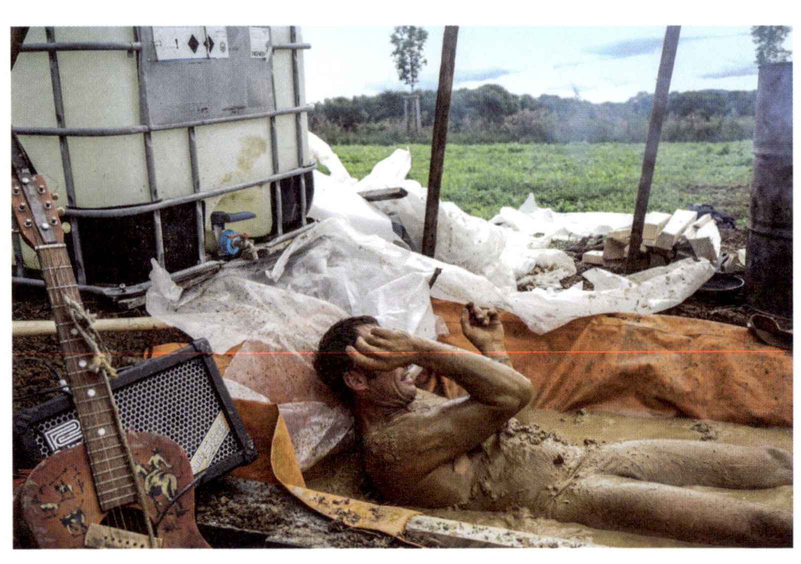

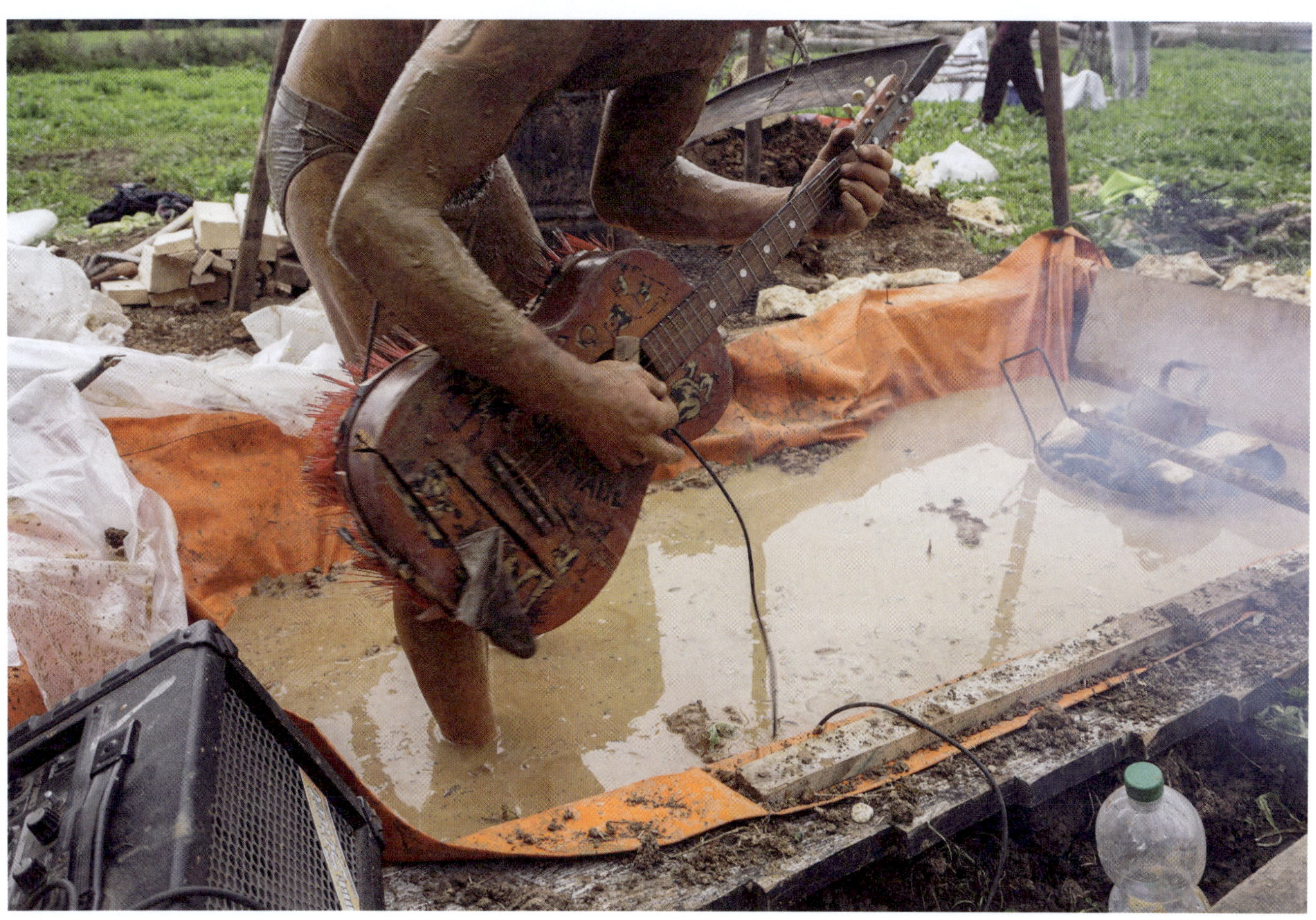

Musikalische Performance anlässlich des Festivals *Interim* in Grabenstetten auf der schwäbischen Alb. Das archaische Schlammbad, mit im Feuer erhitzten Albsteinen und „Gitarrenbürste", inszenierte der Künstler als „keltisches Woodstock" – eine Reminiszenz an den Heidengraben, eine der größten keltischen Siedlungen im südwestdeutschen Raum.
Musical performance for the *Interim* festival in Grabenstetten, Swabian Alps. Set with Alp stones heated by fire and featuring a "guitar brush," this ancient mud bath in Heidengraben, one of the largest Celtic settlements in south-western Germany, had the feel of a Celtic Woodstock.

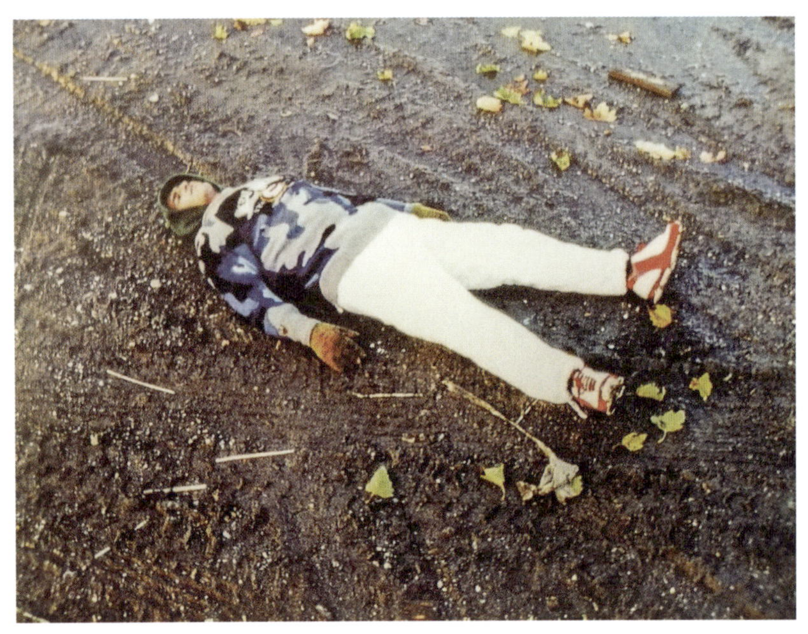

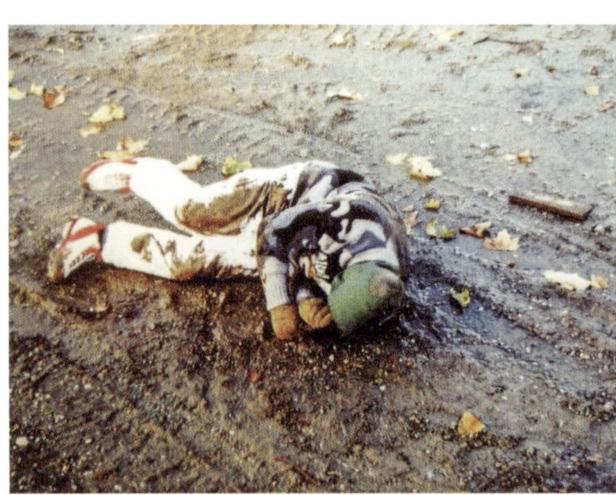

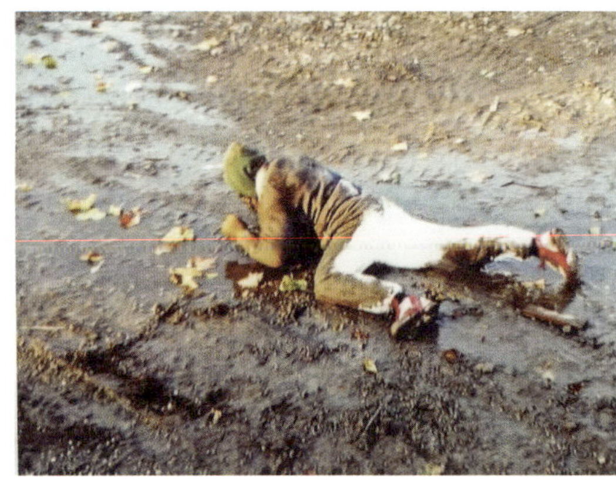

Oktober /
October
2003

Platzwerdung

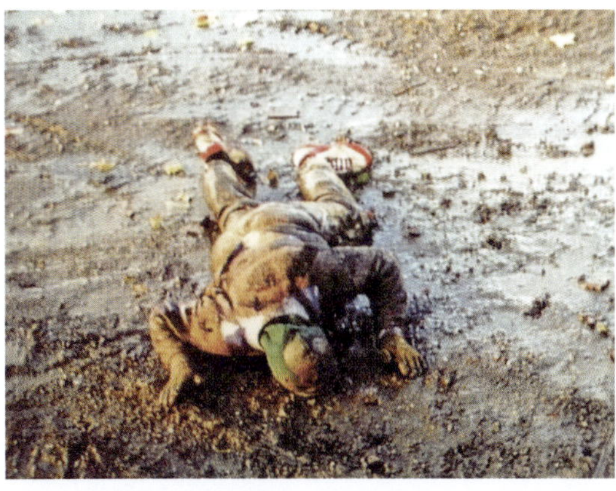

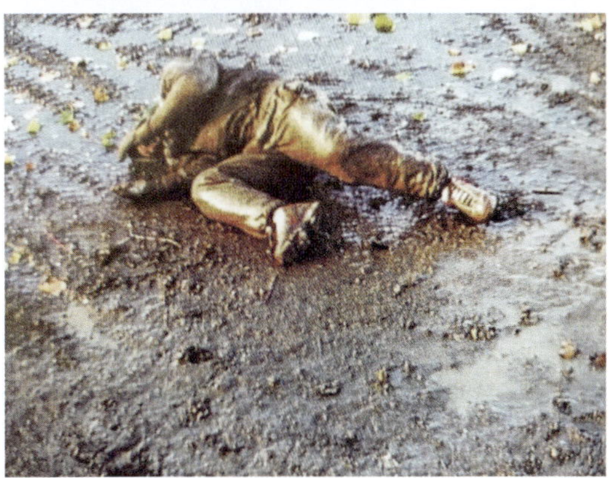

Performance mit der Klasse Micha Ullmann während des Studiums an der Staatlichen Akademie der Bildenden Künste in Stuttgart. Die auf dem Cannstatter Wasen, einem Stuttgarter Festplatz, vorgenommene Performance war der Auftakt für eine Reihe von Aktionen, mittels derer der Künstler den Versuch unternimmt, komplett Eins zu werden mit dem Ort und dem Material.
Performance with the class of Micha Ullmann during the artist's studies at the Academy of Fine Arts in Stuttgart.
The performance conducted at the Cannstatter Wasen festival grounds was the prelude to a series of performances in which the artist endeavored to become entirely one with place and matter.

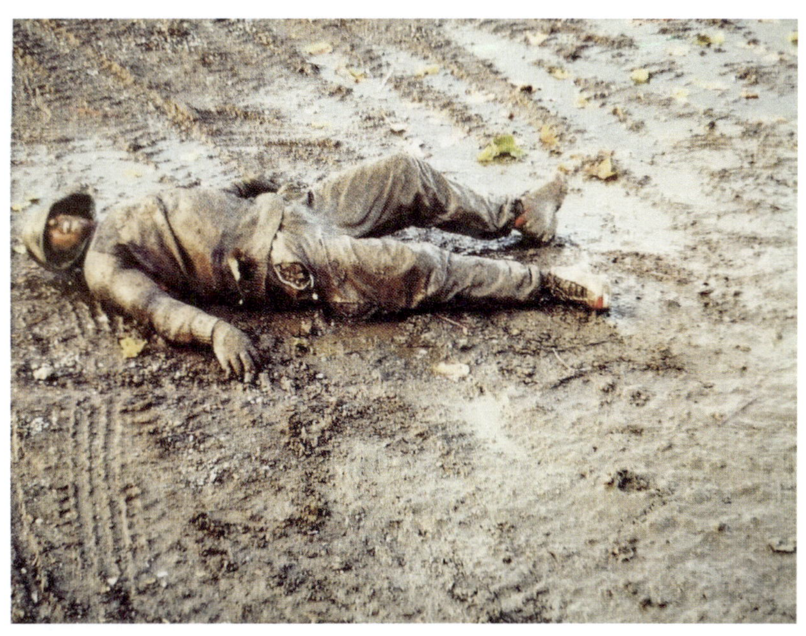

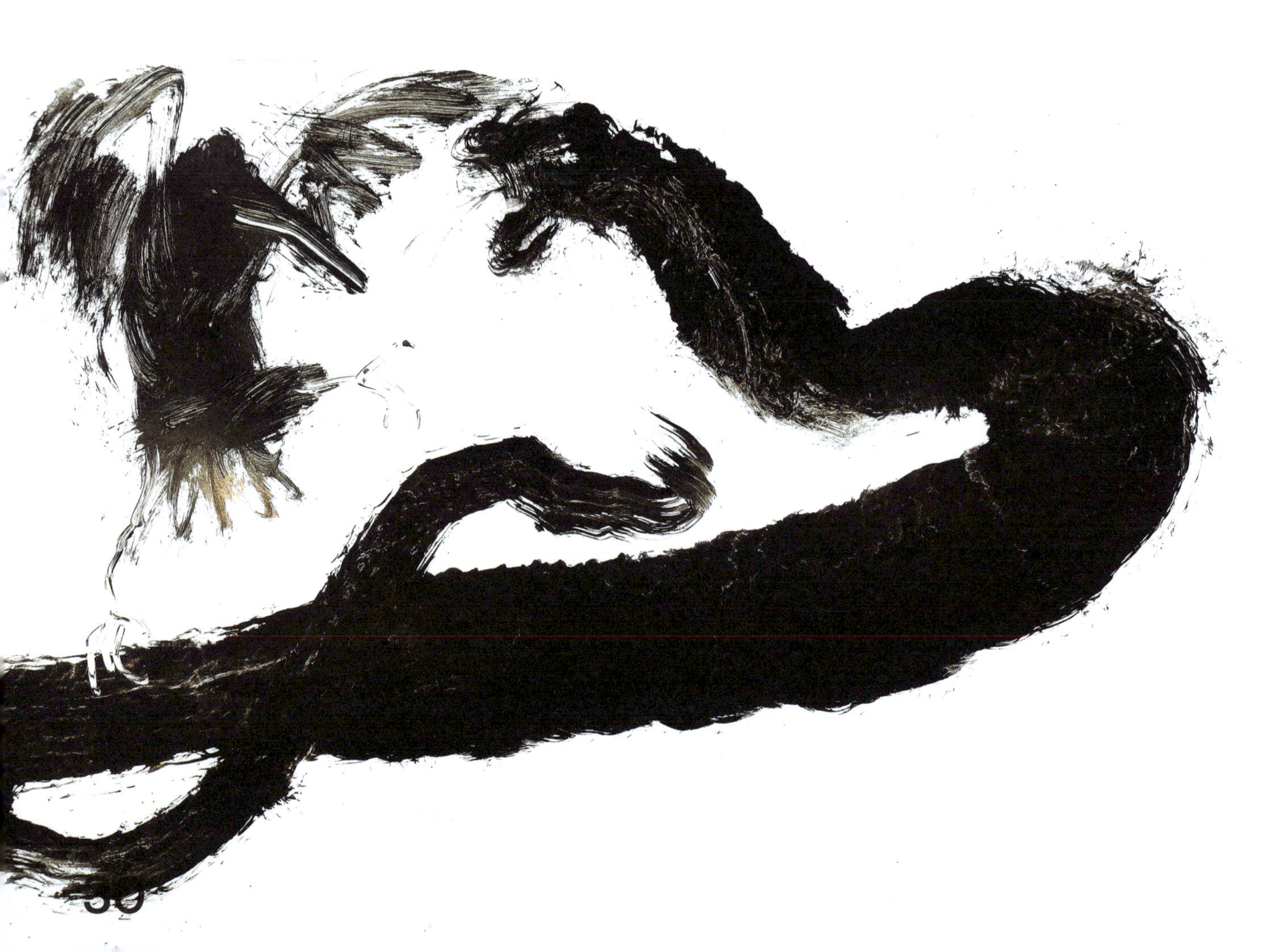

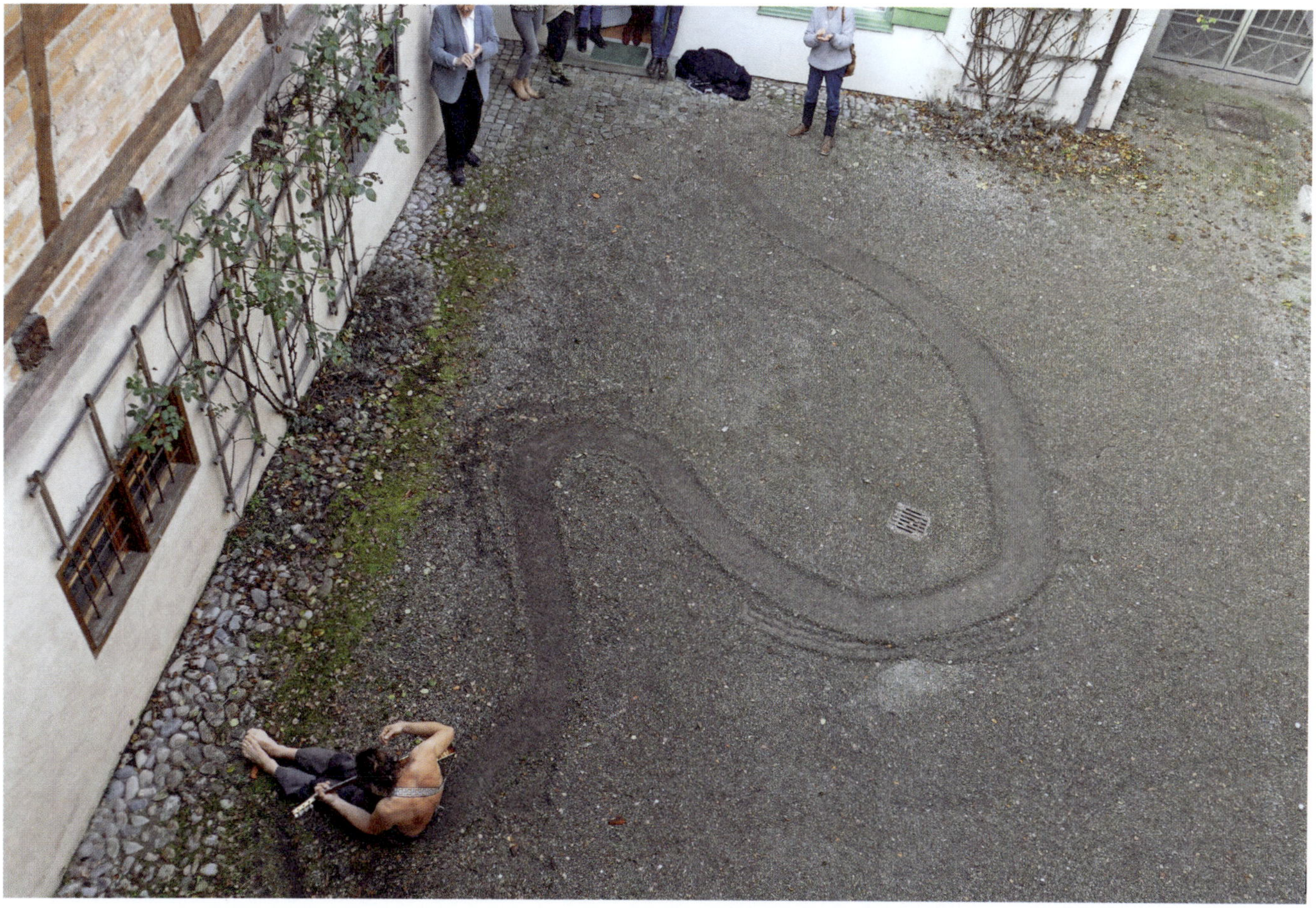

Musikalische Performance zur Vernissage der Ausstellung *Schlangen-Linien*, Galerie in der Badstube, Wangen im Allgäu, am 26. Januar 2020. Der Künstler performte auf dem Boden sitzend, vorwärtsrobbend den *Crawling King Snake*-Blues und hinterließ dabei, zuerst im Ausstellungsraum in ausgestäubtem Mehl und später im Innenhof der Galerie eine Schlagenlinie als Spur.
Musical performance for the vernissage of the exhibition *Schlangen-Linien* (Snake Trail) at Galerie in der Badstube, Wangen im Allgäu, January 26, 2020. The artist performed the *Crawling King Snake* blues while edging forwards as he was sat on the floor. In his wake he left a snake trail, first in the exhibition space with dusted flour and subsequently in the inner courtyard of the gallery.

Januar / January 2020

Crawling King Snake

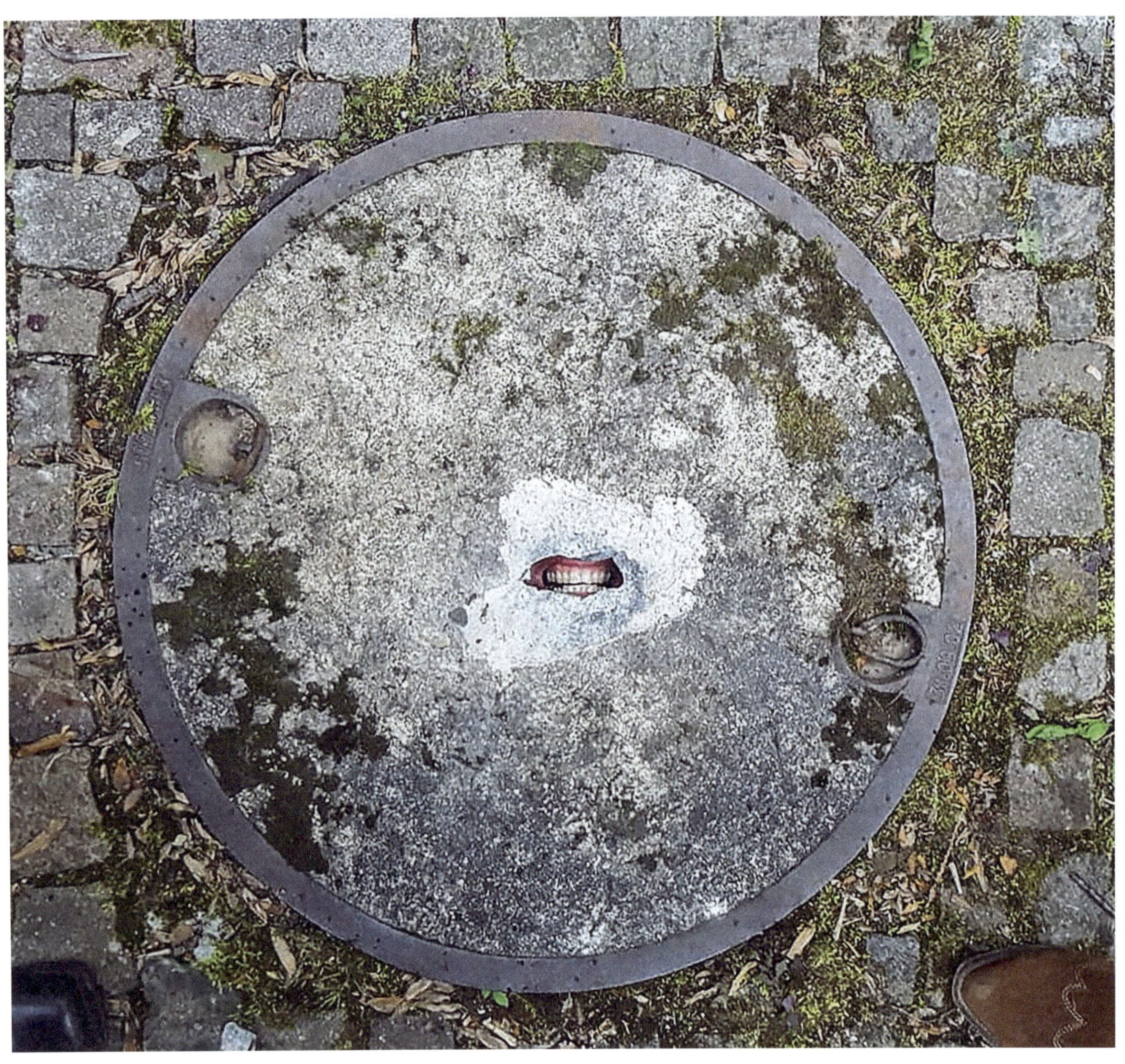

Mai / May 2019

Unterirdisch

Performance zur Vernissage der Ausstellung *Humus. Micha Ullman und seine ehemaligen Studierenden* am 17. Mai 2019, HuMBASE Stuttgart. Anlässlich des 80. Geburtstages von Prof. Micha Ullmann organisierten ehemalige Studierende die Ausstellung *Humus*. Als Hommage an seinen Professor und in Anlehnung an dessen Werk, das sich intensiv mit unterirdischen Räumen befasst, griff Thomas Putze dessen Ansatz auf, indem er vor dem Ausstellungsort HuMBASE hinunter in den Abgrund stieg. Die Performance knüpft auch an seine frühe Performance *Platzwerdung* aus der Studienzeit an (S. 28/29). Das Bild entstand, als der im Untergrund bluesspielende Performer die umstehenden Ausstellungsbesucher um einen Schluck Bier bat.

Performance for the vernissage of the exhibition *Humus: Micha Ullman und seine ehemaligen Studierenden* (Humus: Micha Ullmann and His Former Students) at HuMBASE in Stuttgart, May 17, 2019. For Professor Micha Ullmann's eightieth birthday, former students organized the *Humus* exhibition. As a tribute to his professor and referencing his work addressing subterranean spaces, the artist climbed underground in front of the exhibition location HuMBASE. It tied in with *Platzwerdung* (Becoming Space), an earlier performance from his student days (pp. 28/29). The picture came about just as the underground blues-playing performer asked the surrounding exhibition visitors for a sip of beer.

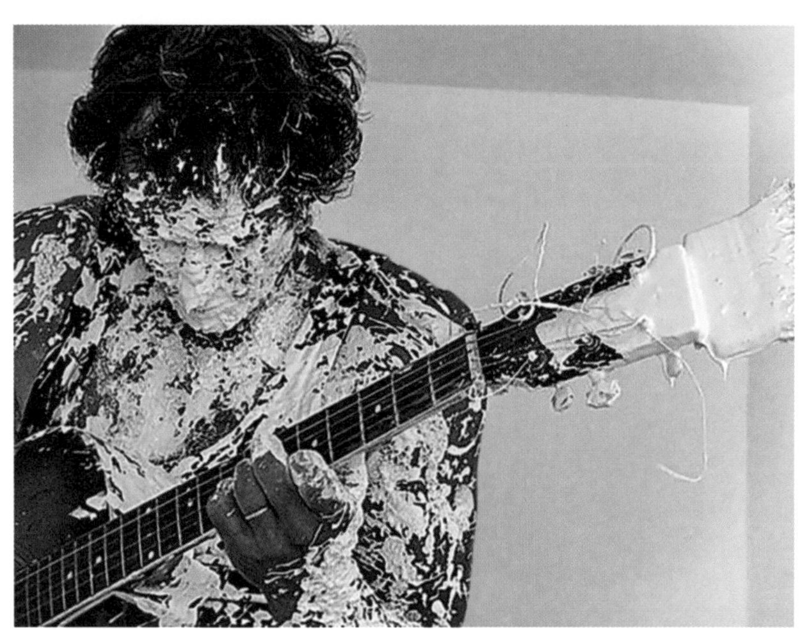

Alles Putze All Things Putze

Werner Pokorny

Alles Putze ist der Titel eines Kataloges aus dem Jahr 2013, der das Werk von Thomas Putze in mehreren Ausstellungen zeigte, und die Auswahl beweist, dass für ihn alle möglichen künstlerischen Ausdrucksformen von der Performance über die Skulptur bis hin zur Zeichnung interessant und in jeder Form, bis hin zum extremen körperlichen Einsatz, wichtig und Gegenstand seines intensiven Engagements sind. In dem vorliegenden Katalog *Putze Performances 2000–2020* konzentriert er sich nun ganz auf die Performance als künstlerisches Ausdrucksmittel.

Als *Säulenheiliger* (Schorndorf 2016, S. 38–41), oder *White Boy Playing the Blues* (Kunstverein Memmingen 2012, S. 37), beim *Klettern auf Solitude* (Schloss Solitude 2002, S. 68) oder als Kletterer und Schwimmer bei der Performance *Biber* (Donaugalerie Tuttlingen 2019, S. 78–81) und vielen weiteren performativen Aktionen zeigt Thomas Putze hohen körperlichen Einsatz, der zum Teil auch an das Limit der Möglichkeiten geht und damit auch als eine inhaltliche Infragestellung die Gefahr des Scheiterns andeutet. Es scheint mir dabei eine besondere Qualität zu sein, dass er uns in seinen Arbeiten als Betrachtende – und oft auch Beteiligte – auf die grundlegenden Fragen „schaffe ich das überhaupt?" oder „wohin führt das?" verweist.

Zu der außerordentlichen Vielfalt der künstlerischen Ansätze von Thomas Putze gehört neben der intensiven Auseinandersetzung mit Performance – und oft damit verbunden – Skulptur, Zeichnung, Malerei und Musik.

In engem Bezug zur Natur entstehen Holzskulpturen, die oft mit den unterschiedlichsten Materialien verbunden sind und ebenso wie seine Malereien und spontanen Zeichnungen das Bild einer komplexen Gedankenwelt wiedergeben.

Alles Putze (All Things Putze) is the title of a catalogue from 2013 featuring the work of Thomas Putze from several exhibitions. The selection of works demonstrates that all possible forms of artistic expression, from performance and sculpture to drawing, are interesting to him and are important and the subject of his intense undertakings in all their forms, including extreme physical exertion. In the current publication, *Putze Performances 2000–2020*, he now focuses entirely on performance as a creative means of expression.

As a *Säulenheiliger* (Stylite; Schorndorf, 2016, pp. 38–41) or *White Boy Playing the Blues* (Kunstverein Memmingen, 2012, p. 37), with *Klettern auf Solitude* (Scaling Solitude; Schloss Solitude, 2002, p. 68) or as a climber and swimmer in the performance *Biber* (Beaver; Donaugalerie Tuttlingen, 2019, pp. 78–81), as well as in many other performative actions, Thomas Putze displays a high level of physical exertion, which at times reaches the limit of what is possible and thus suggests the risk of failure as a questioning of content. It seems to me to be a special quality in his work that we, as observers—and often as participants—are pointed to the fundamental questions of, "Will I even succeed?" and, "Where is this going?"

Wenn Thomas Putze, wie bei der Aktion *Kraftakt I* (Stuttgart 2019, S. 60–67), Mitglieder verschiedener Selbsthilfegruppen mit einem Pinsel, der mit Gewichten belastet war, portraitiert, ist dies als eine geniale, eindrucksvolle Kombination von Zeichnung, Performance und Interaktion zu verstehen.

Musik und Geräusche vielfältigster Art, von der von ihm qualitätvoll gespielten Gitarre bis zur lauten Kettensäge begleiten seine Performances ebenso wie Kabeltrommeln und Stacheldraht.

Micha Ullman spricht in einem Text von 2004 von „unendlicher Phantasie, Humor, Absurdität".

20 Jahre „alles Putze" – es bleibt sicher weiterhin spannend.

The extraordinary diversity of Thomas Putze's approaches includes not only his intense engagement with performance but also the sculpture, drawing, painting, and music that is often associated with it.

In close relation to nature, he creates wooden sculptures, which he often combines with the most diverse materials and which reflect the image of a complex world of thought, just as his paintings and impromptu drawings do.

As in the action *Kraftakt I* (Act of Strength I; Stuttgart, 2019, pp. 60–67), Thomas Putze portraying members of various support groups with a brush laden with weights is to be regarded as a brilliant, impressive combination of drawing, performance, and interaction.

The most multifarious music and sounds—from him playing the guitar to the loud chain saw, likewise a cable reel and barbed wire—accompany his performances in equal measure.

In a text from 2004, Micha Ullman talks of "never-ending imagination, humor, absurdity."

Twenty years of "all things Putze"—no doubt he will continue to excite us.

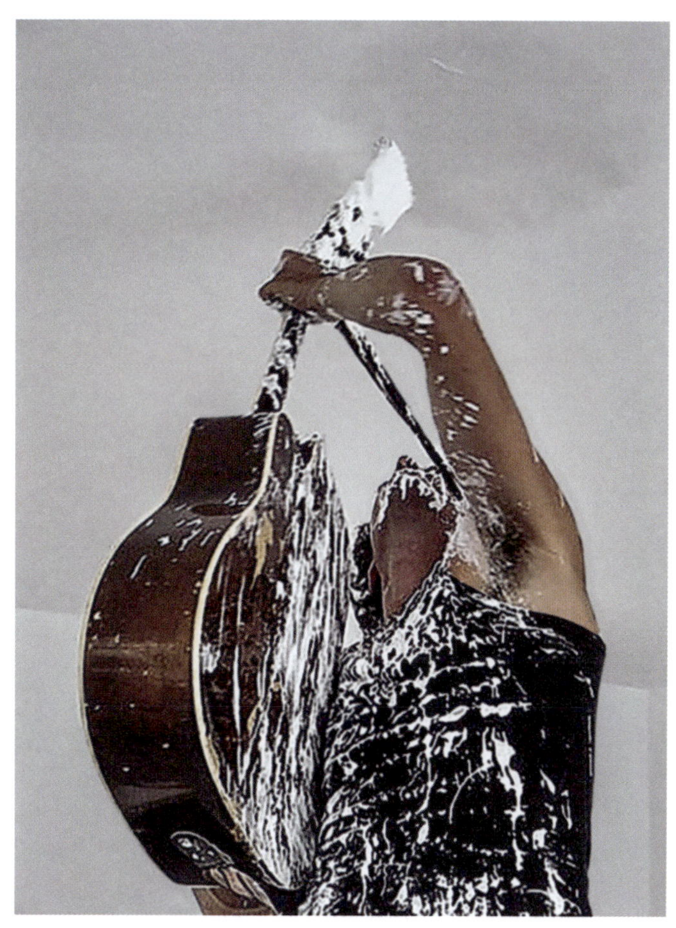

Juni /
June
2012

White Boy
Playing
the Blues

Performance mit Gitarre und weißer Farbe im Kunstverein Memmingen. Gitarre und Blues zählen zu den Grundelementen der Performances von Thomas Putze.
Performance with guitar and white paint at Kunstverein Memmingen. The guitar and the blues are among the fundamental elements of Thomas Putze's performances.

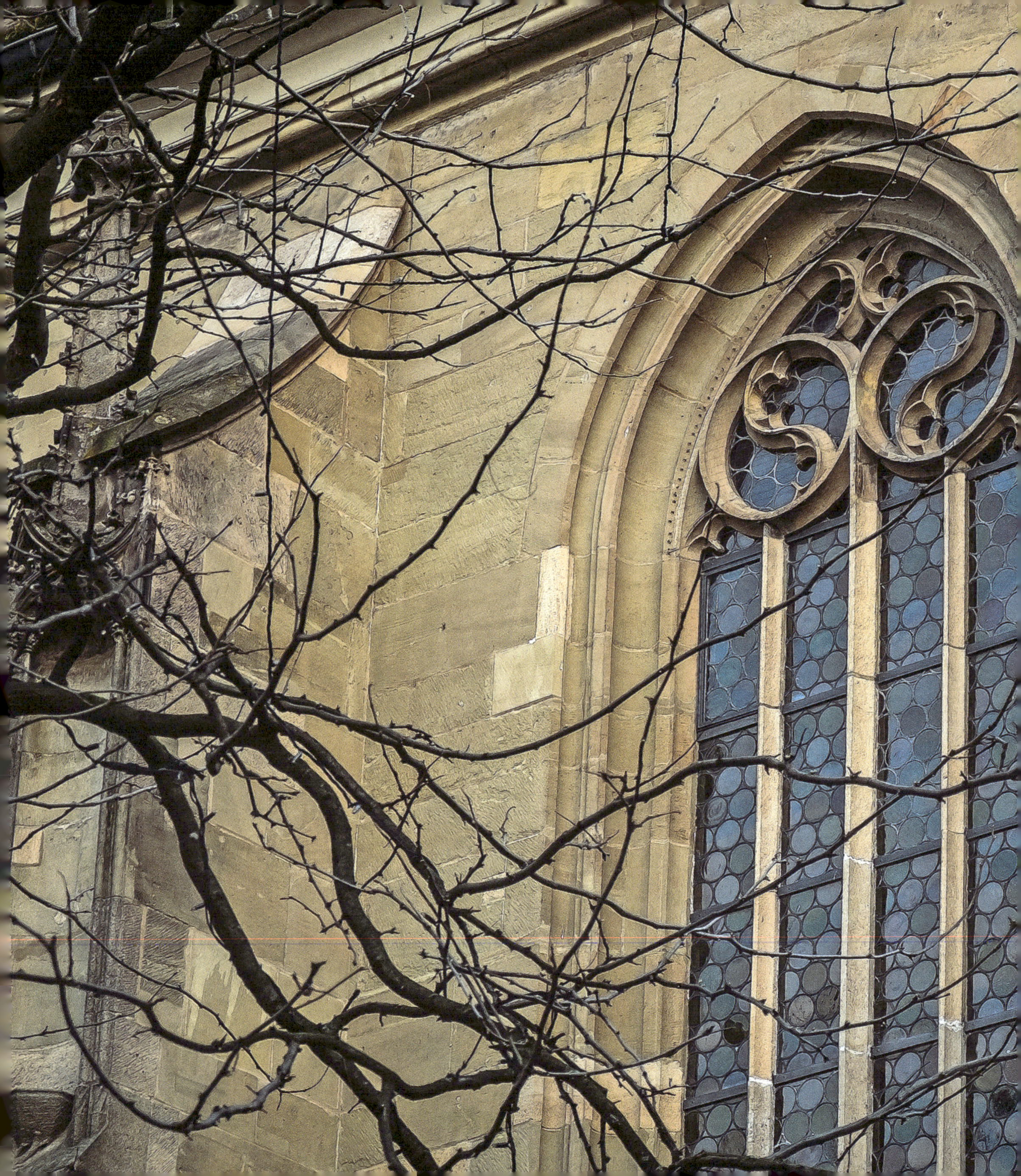

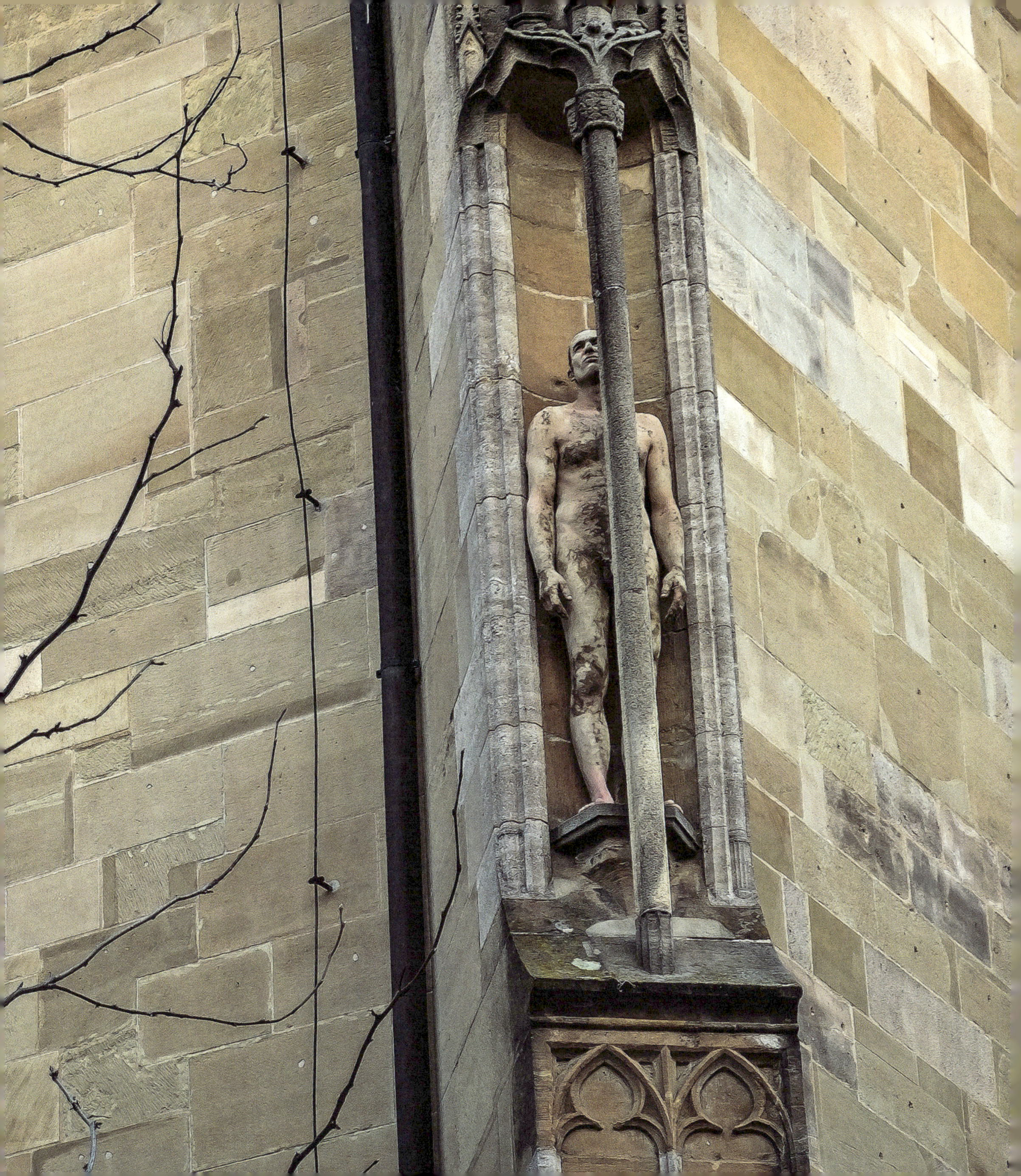

April
2017

Säulenheiliger

Performance an der Schorndorfer Stadtkirche anlässlich des 500-jährigen Reformationsjubiläums, am 9. April 2017. Dreizehn Künstler waren eingeladen worden, die Fassadennischen der Stadtkirche, deren ursprüngliche Skulpturen dem reformatorischen Bildersturm zum Opfer fielen, temporär durch zeitgenössische Werke wieder zu besetzen. Die Künstler waren aufgefordert, mit ihren Beiträgen einen Dialog anzuregen und zur lebendigen, zeitbezogenen und offenen Auseinandersetzung mit dem Thema Reformation beizutragen. Thomas Putze platzierte sich nackt, eingerieben mit Travertinstaub, in der Nische, den Regelverstoß bewusst in Kauf nehmend. Seine Anspielung auf Martin Luthers berühmten Thesenanschlag führte zu ähnlich großer Empörung.

Performance on April 9, 2017, at Schorndorf church for the 500th anniversary of the Reformation. With thirteen artists taking part, the niches on the provincial church's outer facade, whose original sculptures fell victim to the iconoclasm of the Reformation, were temporarily reoccupied by contemporary works. The artists were called upon to provoke a dialogue with their contributions and invite animated, open debate on the Reformation that correlated to the time. Thomas Putze positioned himself naked, rubbed all over with travertine dust, in the niche, willfully condoning a breach of the rules. His play on Martin Luther's famous Theses assault similarly led to great outrage.

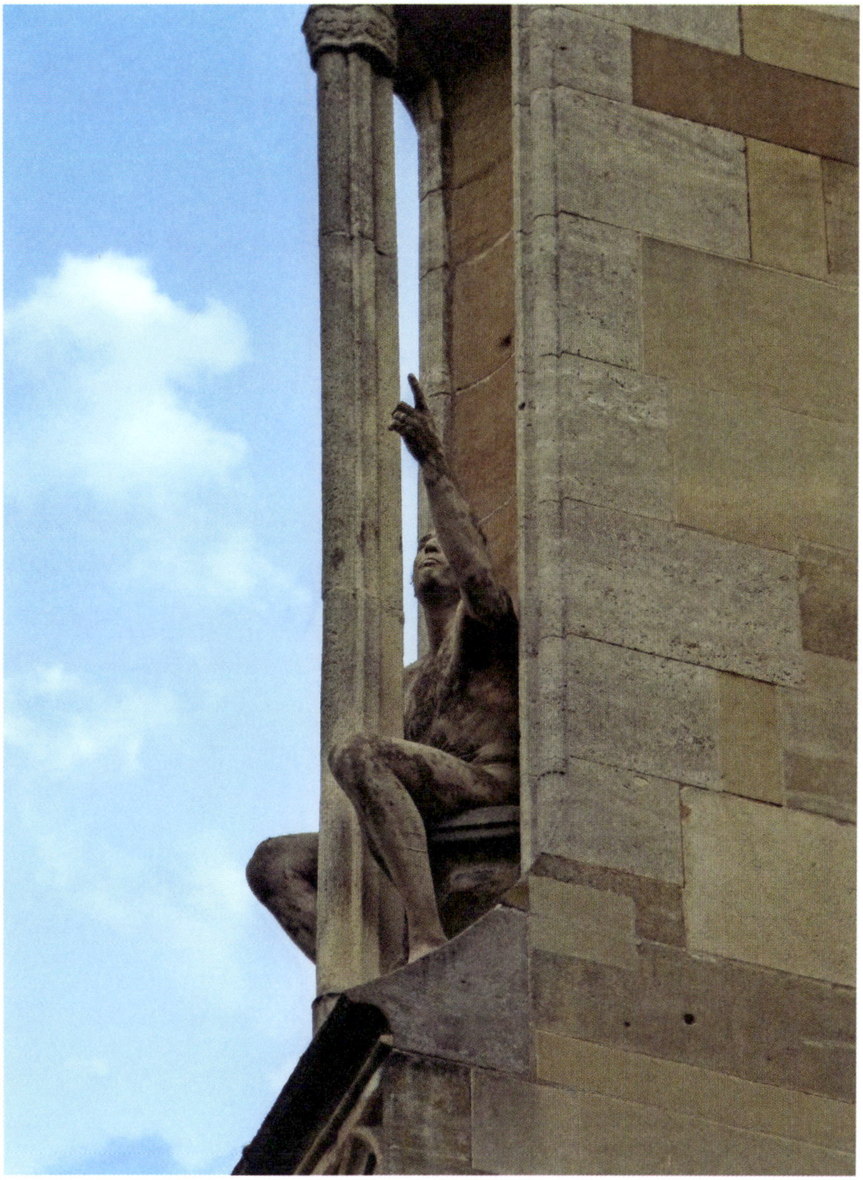

Mitunter im Konflikt – Der Säulenheilige steigt herab

Occasional Conflict—The Stylite Descends

Thomas Erne

Versetzten Sie sich einmal in die Lage der Künstler. Sie sollen in einem Raum ihre Stimme erheben, der so sprechend ist und so starke christliche Botschaften aussendet wie diese Stadtkirche. Jede Bewegung wird hier bedeutungsvoll, jede Regung hat einen symbolischen Mehrwert. In diesem starken Kontext soll der Künstler reden, ohne institutionelle Rückendeckung, ohne öffentliches Amt, ohne Schutz durch einen allgemein akzeptierten Stilbegriff, ohne objektiven Begriff davon, was heute als Kunst gelten kann und was nicht. Er muss seine Stimme erheben als Einzelner und etwas Neues sagen, was sich die Gesellschaft nicht ohne Weiteres selber sagen kann.

Mitunter kann es Konflikte zwischen Kunst und Kirche geben. Thomas Putze war auch bei seiner Performance *Durchzügler* bei uns in der Uni-Kirche in Marburg beinahe nackt und das nicht außen, sondern innen, in der Kirche, sogar im Gottesdienst. Mit einer Plastiktüte als Lendenschurz kletterte er von der Kanzel quer durch den Kirchenraum. Auch in Marburg gab es Diskussionen. Der Gottesdienst war am nächsten Sonntag sogar das Tagesgespräch in der Mensa. […]
Trotzdem finde ich Thomas Putzes Performance in Schorndorf theologisch die stärkste Arbeit im Skulpturenprojekt 2017. Ich habe bei seiner Arbeit begriffen, warum es zu einem Ikonoklasmus der Skulpturen im 16. Jahrhundert kam. Sie waren schlicht überflüssig geworden. Die *communio sanctorum*, die im Glaubensbekenntnis bekannt wird – ich glaube an die heilige christliche Kirche, die Gemeinschaft der Heiligen – wird zur *congregatio sanctorum*. Die Heiligen werden in der Reformation verinnerlicht, ins Innere der Kirche und ins Innere der Frömmigkeit übersetzt, von Statuen in den Geist der Gemeinde, die sich in der Kirche um Wort und Sakrament versammelt. Die Heiligen an der Schorndorfer Stadtkirche sind 1530 von

Put yourself in the place of artists. They are expected to speak out in a room as meaningful and communicative with strong Christian messages as this provincial church. Every movement becomes significant here; every impulse has an added symbolic value. Within this intense context, the artist is to speak without institutional backing, without public office, without the protection of generally accepted stylistic notions, without an objective definition of what can or cannot be considered art today. He must speak out as an individual and say something new that society cannot readily say to itself.
Sometimes conflicts can arise between art and the Church. Thomas Putze too was at our University Church in Marburg for his performance *Durchzügler* (Passage Migrant), all but naked, and not outside, but inside, actually in the church, during service. Wearing a plastic bag as a loin cloth, he climbed down from the pulpit and clambered across the church interior. And there was talk about it in Marburg. The church service was even the topic of the day in the refectory the following Sunday. […]
But for all that, I find Thomas Putze's performance in Schorndorf for the 2017 Sculpture Project the strongest work theologically speaking. With his work

ihrem Sockel gestiegen und in die Kirche eingewandert. Sie wurden zu Menschen aus Fleisch und Blut, wie du und ich. Sie sind es nicht im Blick auf sich selbst, ihre Leistungen, ihre Titel, ihr Vermögen, ihr polizeiliches Führungszeugnis, aber sie sind es *coram Deo*: wenn sie ihr Dasein im Horizont der Anerkennung durch Gott weiten lassen, *sola gratia*, aus Gnade allein.
Thomas Putze zeigt uns diesen Weg der Heiligen, von der Säule ins Innere, in die Kirche und in die Innerlichkeit. Er wird noch einmal zu Stein und steigt dann herab, um am Sonntag, im Gottesdienst in der Kirche, die umfassendste Weitung seines Daseins zu erleben, die Schorndorf seinen Bürgern zu bieten hat: Die Weitung des Daseins, hinein in das Heilige, in die Gegenwart Gottes.

[Auszug aus der Rede: „Auf der Schwelle – Kirche und Kunst begegnen sich“, Stadtkirche Schorndorf, Skulpturen 2017, Finissage]

I realized how the iconoclasm of sculptures came about in the sixteenth century. They had simply become superfluous. The *communio sanctorum* recognized in the Apostles' Creed—I believe in the holy Christian Church, the communion of saints—became *congregatio sanctorum*. During the Reformation the saints were internalized, translated into the interior of the church and inward piety, from statues into the spirit of the congregation, who gathered in the church around The Word and the sacrament. In 1530 the hallowed at the church in Schorndorf rose from their pedestals and entered the church. They became people, of flesh and blood, like you and me. But not as they view themselves, their achievements, their titles, their possessions, their certificate of good conduct but rather *coram deo*, if they expand their existence within the horizon of God's recognition *sola gratia*, by grace alone.
Thomas Putze shows us the holy way, from the columns to the interior, to the church and inwardness. He becomes stone once more then descends in order to experience the most extensive expansion of his existence that Schorndorf has to offer its citizens during the Sunday church service: the expansion of existence, into the sacred, into the presence of God.

[Excerpt from the speech "Auf der Schwelle—Kirche und Kunst begegnen sich" (On the Threshold—An Encounter between Church and Art), Stadtkirche Schorndorf, 2017 Sculpture Project, finissage]

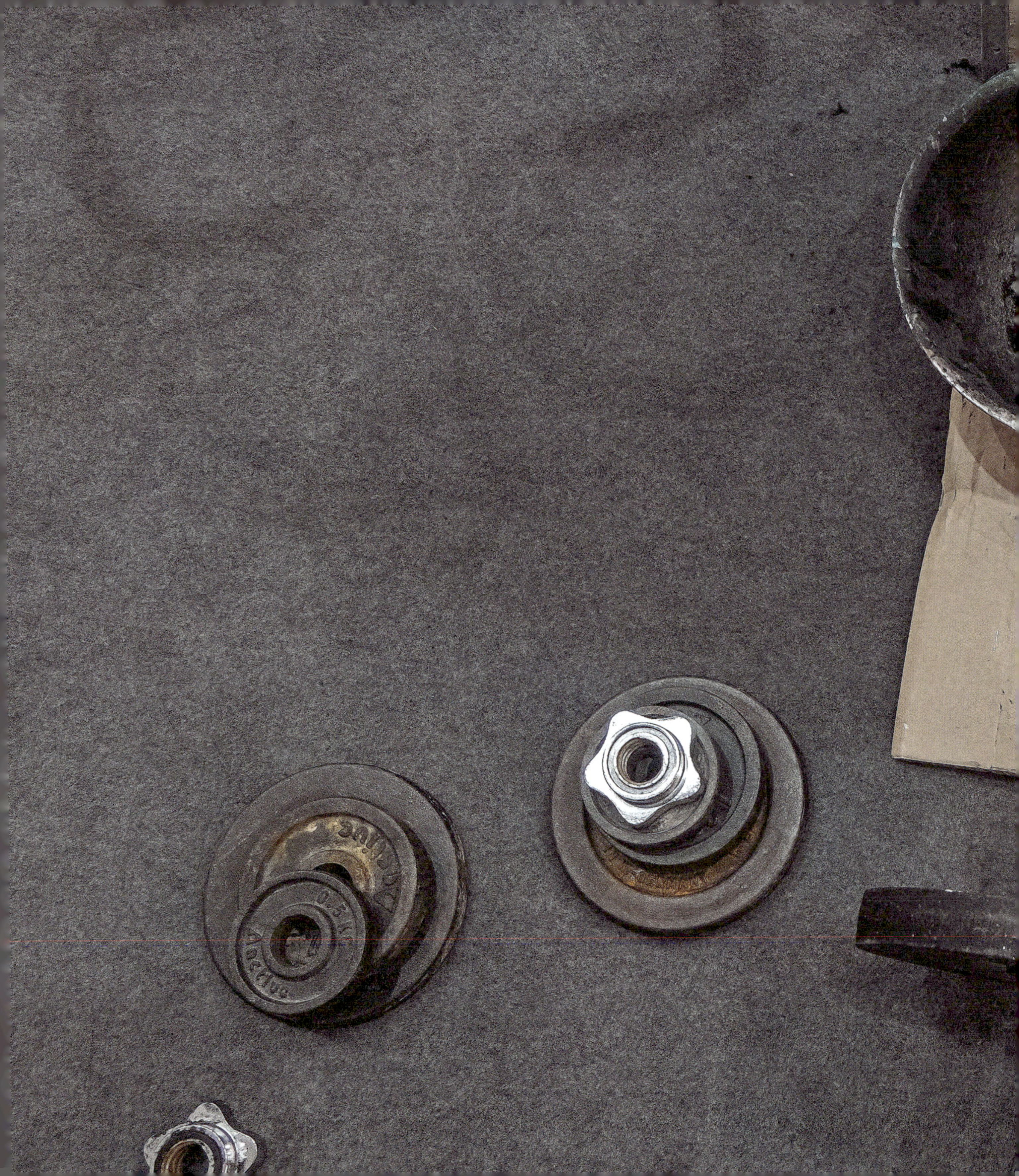

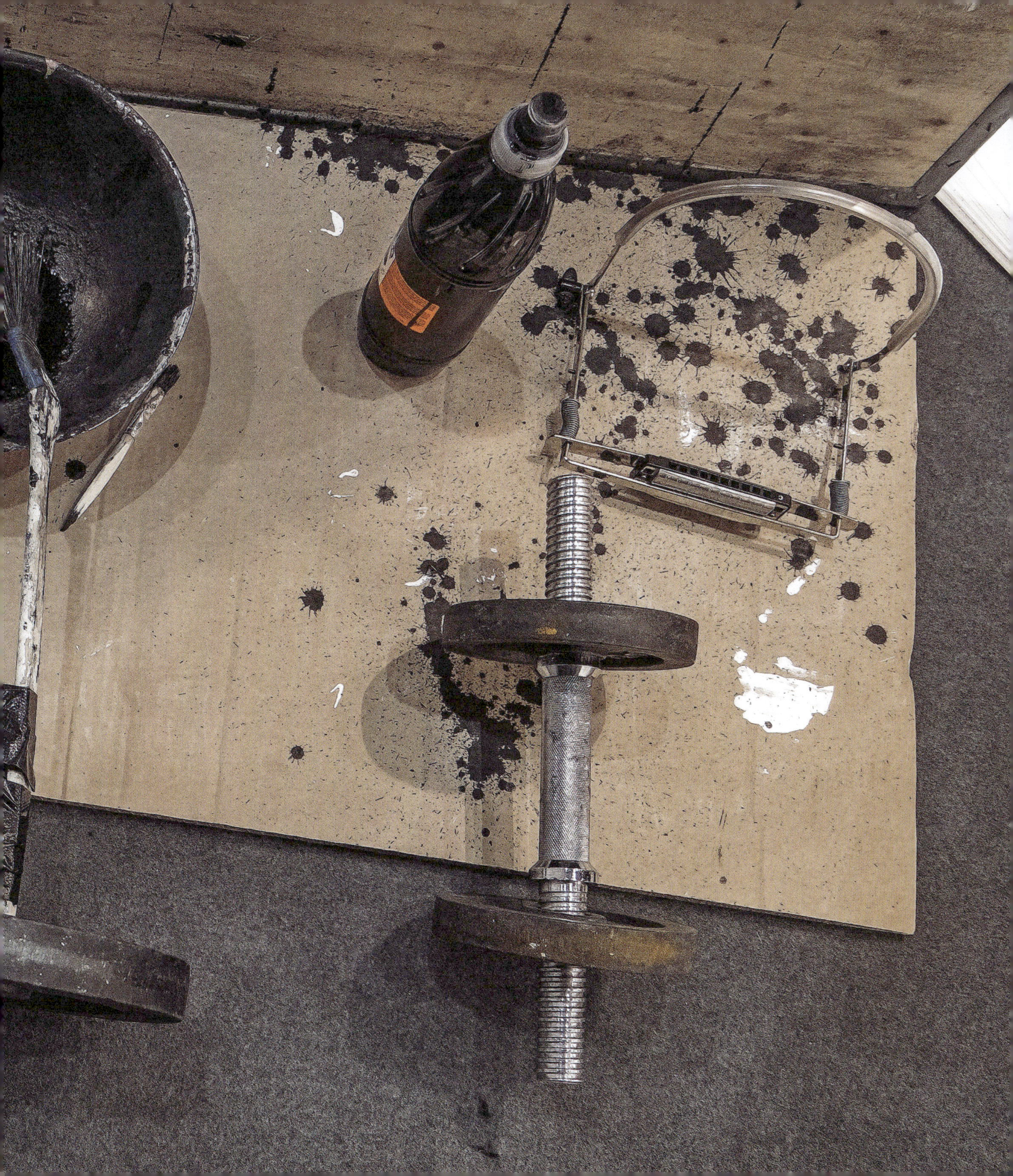

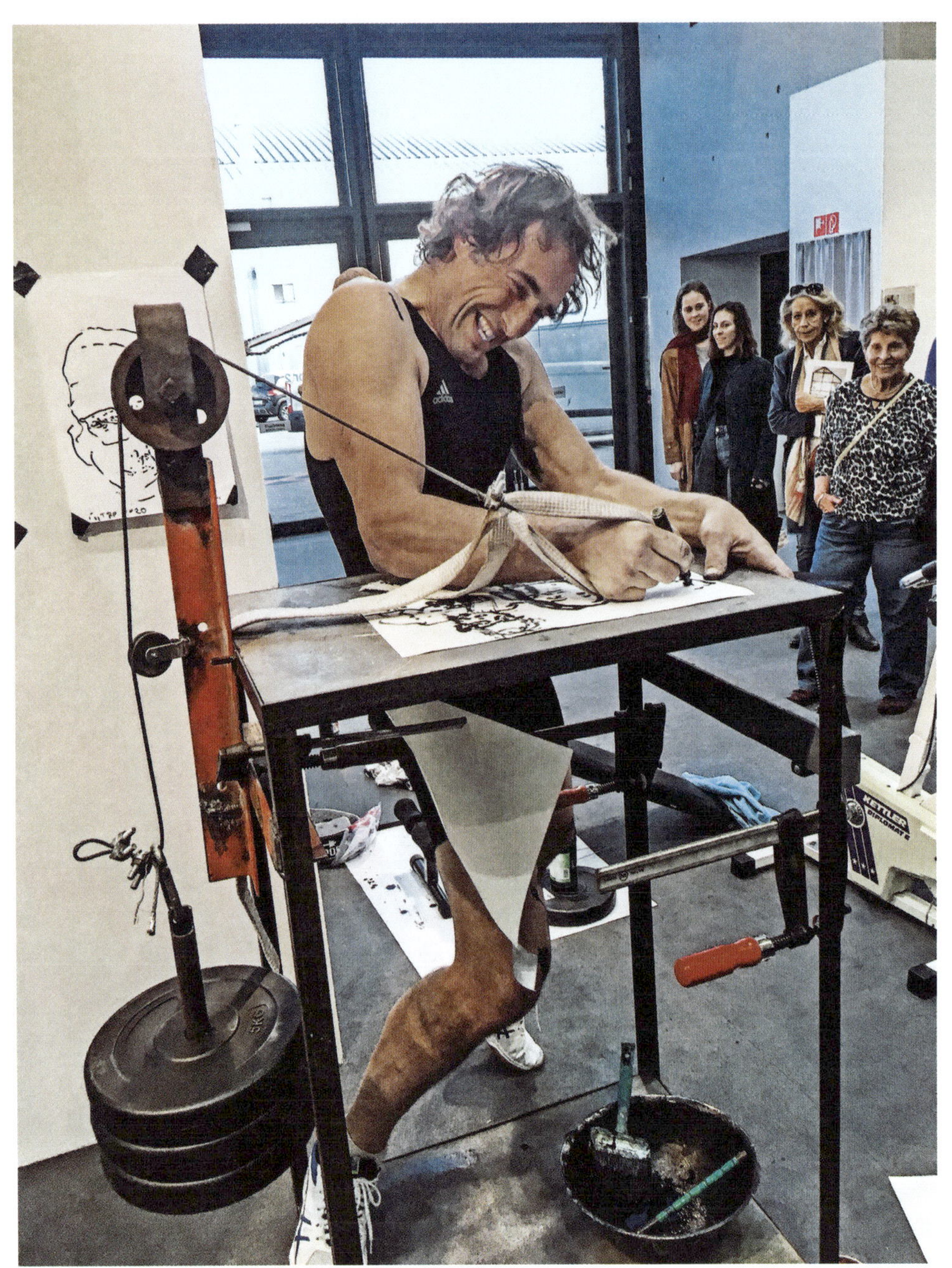

Warum einfach, wenn's auch schwer geht?

Why make it easy when it can also be difficult?

Marko Schacher

Subjektive Anmerkungen zur Kunst des Thomas Putze

Subjective comments on the art of Thomas Putze

Wenn die Michelangelo zugeschriebene Aussage „Eine Skulptur ist gut, wenn man sie einen Berg hinunter rollen kann und nichts abbricht“ stimmt, dann sind Thomas Putzes Figuren richtig schlecht. „Rollen“ kann man sie in der Regel gar nicht, dazu sind die aus Ästen, bearbeiteten Baumstämmen und zahlreichen metallenen Fundstücken zusammengesetzten Skulpturen viel zu widerspenstig und zu unförmig. Wenn Michelangelo Buonarroti mit seinem (später vom Esslinger Bildhauer Otto Baum übernommenen) Satz aber den Sinn der Allansichtigkeit betonen wollte, dann dürfen Putzes Figuren stolz den Finger und die Brust heben.

In der Regel fordern uns Putzes Skulpturen zur Umrundung auf und wollen aus allen Winkeln betrachtet werden. Meist motivieren sie auch zur Berührung. Zu den optischen Qualitäten gesellen sich haptische Abenteuer: Glatte Oberflächen von Sessel-Sprungfedern stehen gleichberechtigt neben rauen Flächen von alten, verrosteten Hantelgewichten und gesplitterten Fasern von Naturhölzern aller Art. Selbst wenn Putzes Agglomerate manchmal auf Sockeln präsentiert werden, haben sie mit den klassischen Skulpturen der achso hehren Kunstwelt wenig gemeinsam. Bei Putze und seinem Publikum gibt es flache Hierarchien. Auch die Grenzen zwischen E- und U-Kunst gibt es bei ihm nicht. Das bezeugen zahlreiche Präsentationen an für Kunstausstellungen eher unüblichen Orten, sein Mitwirken in publikumsnahen Projekträumen, Führungen, Workshops und Kursen für Kinder – und nicht zuletzt seine mit Unikaten bemalten Platten-Cover. Den rohen Skulpturen sieht man ihre Gemachtheit, die vorgenommenen Bearbeitungen mit der Kettensäge, der Axt und dem Stechbeitel an. Farben spielen eine untergeordnete Rolle. Die Welt da draußen eins zu eins, realistisch abzubilden, ist keine Aufgabe, der sich Thomas Putze stellen möchte. Gott sei Dank.

If the statement attributed to Michelangelo that “a sculpture is good if it can be rolled down a hill and nothing breaks off” is correct, then Thomas Putze’s figures are really bad. Normally they cannot be “rolled” at all; the sculptures, made up of branches, processed tree trunks, and numerous found metal objects, are much too unruly and misshapen for that. If the intention of Michelangelo Buonarroti’s phrase (later adopted by the sculptor Otto Baum from Esslingen) was to emphasize the sense of seeing in the round, then Putze’s figures may proudly raise a finger as well as their chests. As a rule, Putze’s sculptures invite us to walk around them and are intended to be observed from all angles; they also often prompt us to touch them. Visual qualities combine with haptic adventure: smooth surfaces of sofa springs stand on an equal footing alongside rough surfaces of old, rusted dumbbells and splintered fibers from natural woods of every description. Even when Putze’s assemblages are occasionally presented on pedestals, they have little in common with the classical sculptures of the oh so noble world of art. The hierarchy between Putze and his public is a flat one; there are also no boundaries for him between serious, esoteric art and art for entertainment’s sake. This is attested to by the numerous presentations in locations that are rather unusual for exhibitions, collaborating

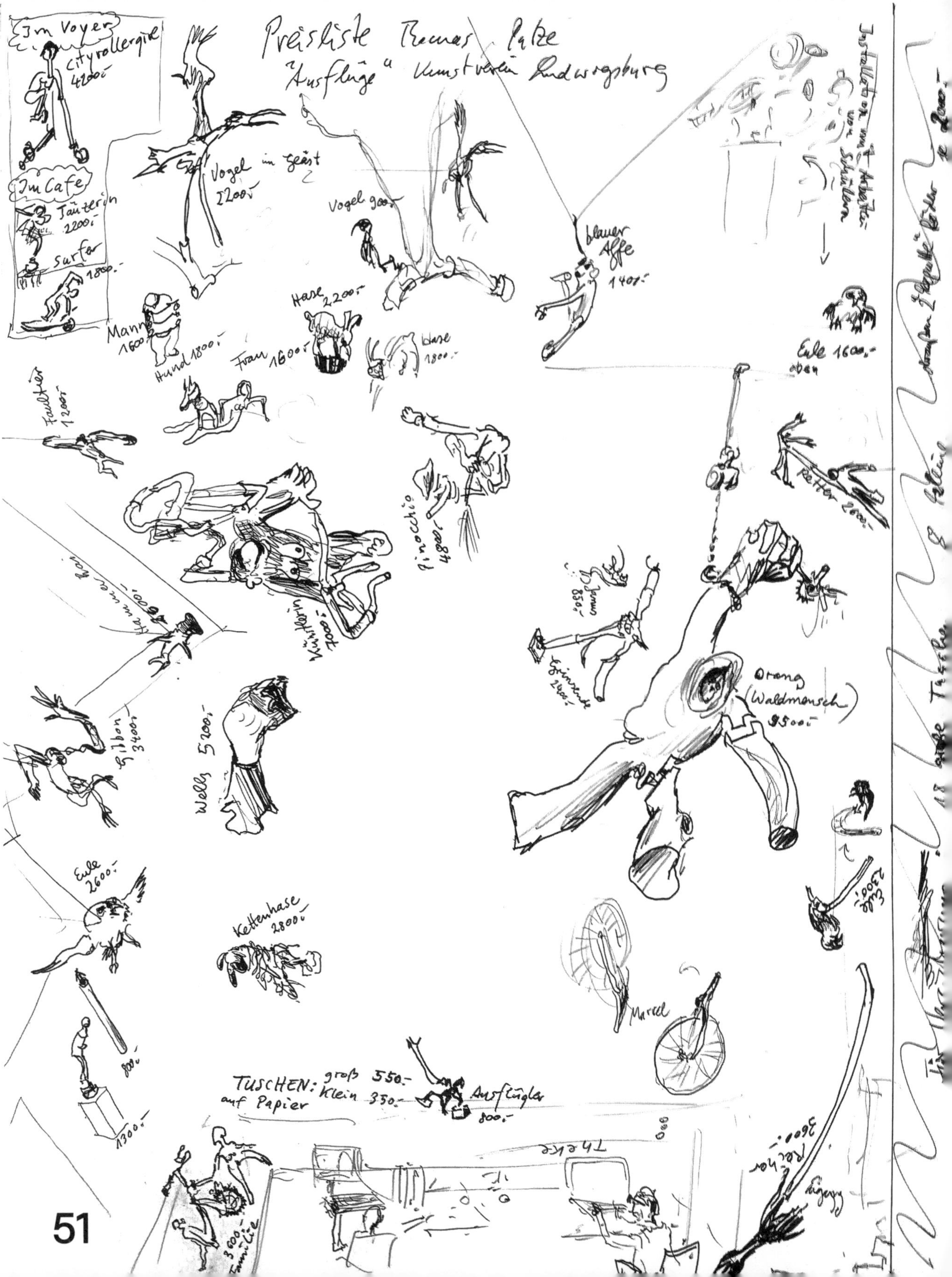

Preisliste Thomas Putze
"Ausflüge" Kunstverein Ludwigsburg

Im Voyer
cityrollergirl 4200.-

Im Cafe
Tänzerin 2200.-
Surfer 1800.-

Vogel im Geäst 2200.-
Vogel 900.-
blauer Affe 1400.-
Mann 1600.-
Hund 1800.-
Hase 2200.-
Frau 1600.-
Hase 1800.-
Eule 1600.- oben
Faultier 1200.-
Pinocchio 4800.-
Künstlerin 7000.-
Retter 2600.-
Jonas 850.-
Grimmige 2400.-
Orang (Waldmensch) 9500.-
Wells 5200.-
Gibbon 3400.-
Eule 2600.-
Kettenhase 2800.-
Eule 2300.-
Marcel
800.-
1300.-
TUSCHEN: groß 550.- klein 350.- auf Papier
Ausflügler 800.-
Theke
Reiher 3600.-
Eingang
3600.- Familie

Installation von 8 Arbeiten von Schülern

51

Preisliste zur Ausstellung / price list for the exhibition Vogelfrei (Outdwell), 2010, Kunstverein Germersheim

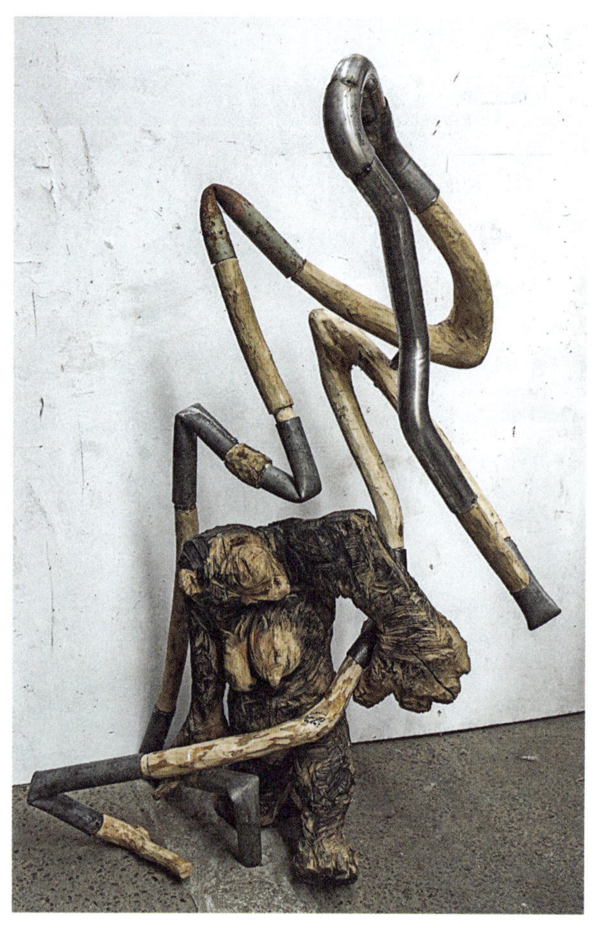

Doppel- oder gar Dreifachbegabungen sind bei Bildenden Künstlern keine Seltenheit. Trotzdem verwundert es, mit welcher Leichtigkeit Thomas Putze seine Zeichnungen und Malereien zu Papier bringt, egal ob er sie in Blei, Kohle, Tusche oder in Öl ausführt. Die Originale seiner eigenhändig, meist mit Bleistift oder Kugelschreiber zu Papier gebrachten Preislisten sind bei seinen Ausstellungen begehrte Sammlerstücke. Manchmal erkennt man nicht genau, ob das gezeichnete Federvieh ein Adler oder eine Krähe ist, oder ob der ver-

in project spaces that audiences can easily relate to, workshops and courses for children, and—not least—his record covers painted with one-offs.
The raw sculptures disclose their constructed character, the workmanship undertaken with the chain saw, axe, and chisel. Colors play a subordinate role.
To realistically represent the world out there, one to one, is not a task Thomas wishes to undertake. Thank goodness.
Double, even triple, talents among fine artists are not uncommon. Nevertheless, it is astonishing the lightness with which

meintliche Hund nicht eher ein Bär ist. Dafür aber ist eindeutig zu sehen, dass das gezeichnete oder gemalte Tier mutig oder ängstlich, verklemmt oder frech ist. Seine Tiere haben Charakter! Es sind individuelle Wesen wie wir Menschen!

Vielleicht ist Thomas Putze aber als Performer am allerbesten. Insider wissen längst, dass Putze seine Vernissagen und/oder Finissagen mit eigenwilligen Performances ergänzt. Ich selbst habe den Künstler beispielsweise im zum Käfig umgebauten Glastrakt im Neubau II der Stuttgarter Kunstakademie als Affe herumtoben sehen (2004), auf den Spuren von Jesus halbnackt und mutig bei der Verleihung des Kunstpreises der Evangelischen Landeskirche über die Sitzbänke von St. Amandus in Bad Urach balancierend, kriechend und kletternd erlebt (2012) und als lebenden Tannenbaum mit Plastiktüten-Beschmückung durch die unterirdische Einkaufspassage am Stuttgarter Hauptbahnhof tingeln sehen (2014, S. 100/101). Besucher von Putze-Präsentationen haben ihn bereits als Musiker erlebt, der die Bodenbretter des Ausstellungsraums herausreißt und diese zur Gitarre umfunktioniert, als musizierenden Cowboy, der ein

Thomas Putze brings his drawings and paintings to paper, whether realized with pencil, charcoal, ink, or oil. Even at his exhibitions, the original copies of his price lists, which he inscribed by hand mostly in pencil or ballpoint pen, are coveted collector's items.
Sometimes it is hard to decipher whether the feathered creature he drew is an eagle or a crow, or whether the supposed dog is not rather a bear. But for all this, it is clear to see that the animal he has drawn or painted is bold or fearful, inhibited or impertinent. His animals have character! They are individual beings, just as us humans!

But perhaps Thomas Putze is at his very best as a performer. Insiders have long known that Putze endows the opening or closing of his exhibitions with idiosyncratic performances. I, myself, for example, have seen the artist as a rampaging ape in a cage converted from the glass annex in the Neubau II wing of the Stuttgart Art Academy (2004), in the footsteps of Jesus balancing, crawling, and climbing half naked and spirited over the pews of St. Amandus in Bad Urach on receiving the Protestant Regional Church Art Prize (2012), and as a living fir tree adorned with plastic bags meandering though the subterranean shopping arcade at Stuttgart's

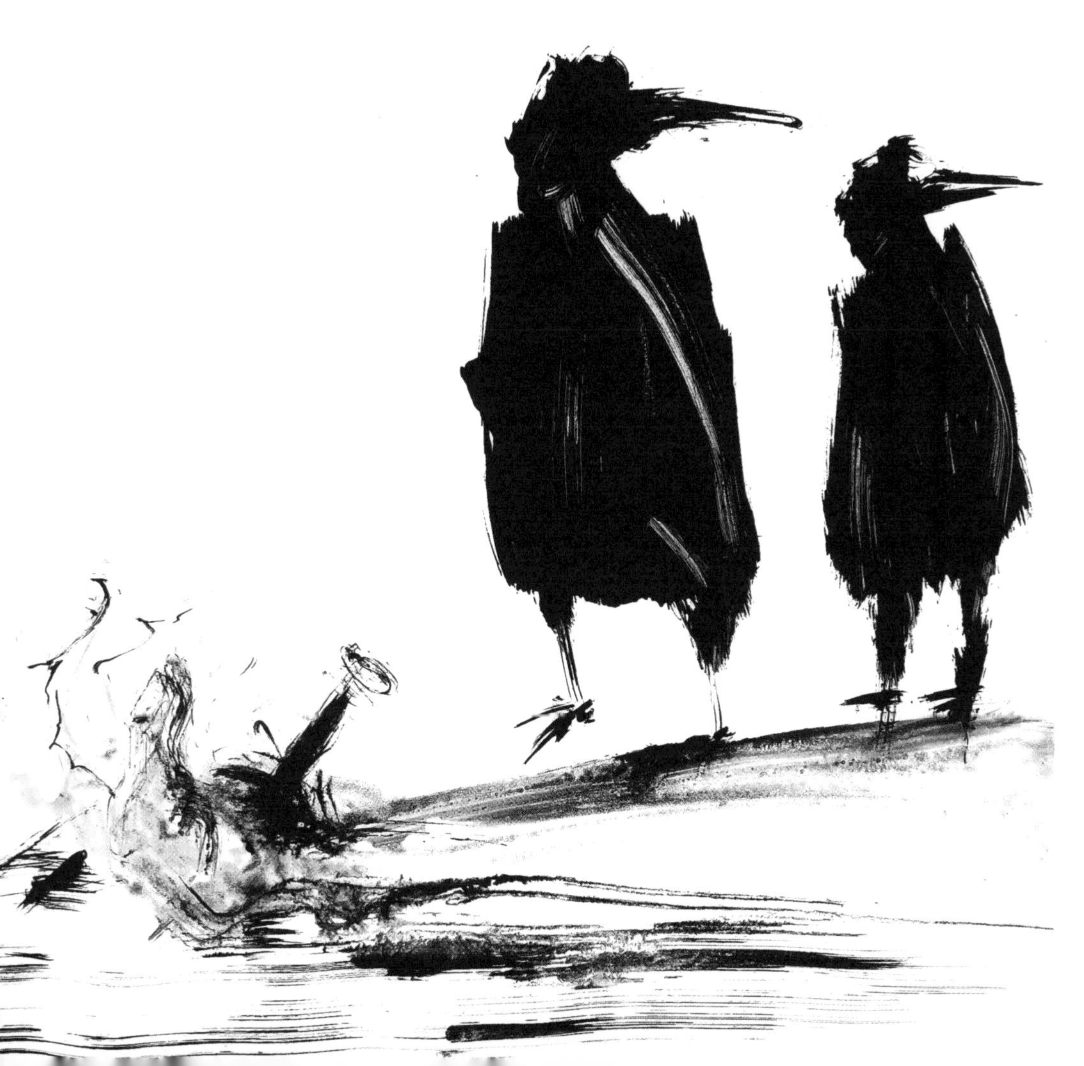

Hometrainer-Fahrrad reitet, oder als Gitarre spielenden Ganzkörper-Kehrwochen-Putzlappen, der hoppelnd den Ausstellungsraum wischt.
Oft geht Thomas Putze bei seinen Performances an Grenzen und lotet die Extreme seiner körperlichen Kräfte aus. Unter dem Titel *Lange Leine* ließ sich Thomas Putze im April 2019 zum Beispiel im Foyer des Theaters Rampe, welches zugleich das abendliche Depot der Stuttgarter Zahnradbahn ist, mit allerhand Kabeln und Elektromüll überschütten, so dass man ihn selbst kaum noch sah (S. 86/87). Mikrofone und Tonabnehmer übertrugen die Geräusche seiner körperlichen Anstrengung und die Bewegungen der Kabel in die Laptops und Sound-Maschinen der Musiker Günter Rolle und Michael Fiedler, die daraus elektronische Live-Beats bastelten. Zur Finissage der Gruppenschau *Mitspieler* der Galerie Schlichtenmaier

Main Station (2014, pp. 100/101). Those who have visited Putze's performances already know him as a musician who rips up the floorboards of the exhibition room and repurposes them as a guitar, as a cowboy making music while riding an exercise bike, or as a guitar-playing life-size cleaning cloth hopping around, wiping the exhibition space as he goes. Thomas Putze frequently pushes boundaries during his performances and plumbs the depths of his own physical strengths. In April 2019, for example, in the foyer of Theatre Rampe, the overnight depot of the Stuttgart rack railway, Thomas Putze had all sorts of cables and electrical waste tipped over him under the title *Lange Leine* (Long Leash), so much so that he was almost no longer visible (pp. 86/87). Microphones and pickups transmitted the sounds of his physical struggles and the movements of the cables to

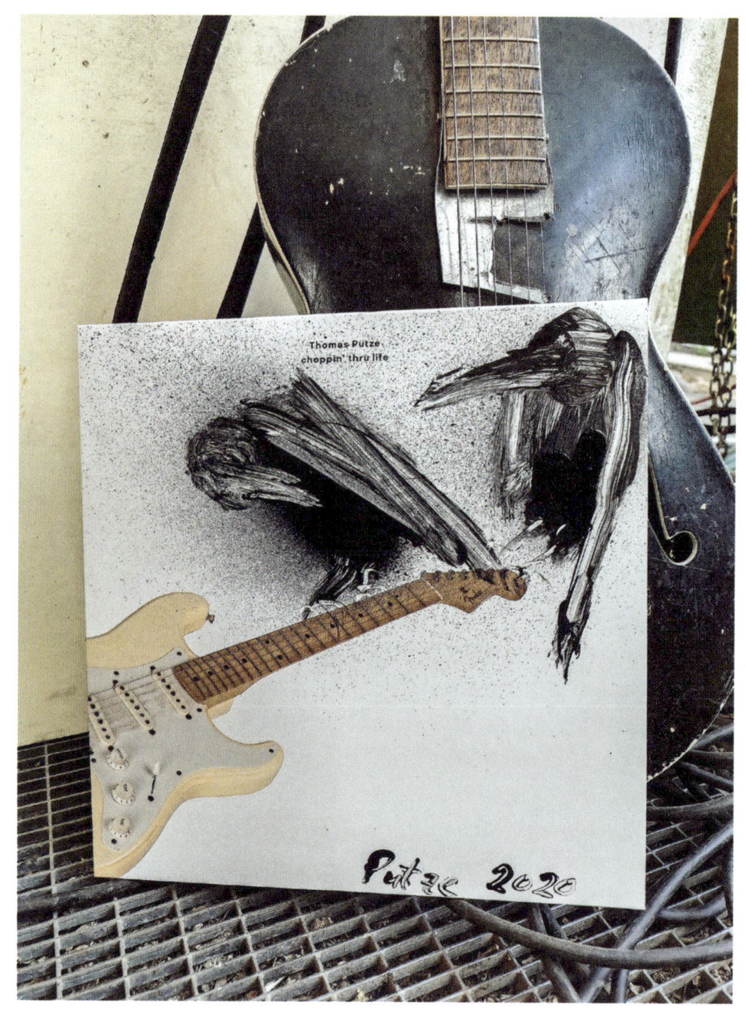
Thomas Putze
choppin' thru life
Putze 2020

im Schloss Dätzingen in Grafenau wiederum hatte Putze eine Performance mit dem Titel *Das Schloss* angekündigt. Vor Ort offenbarte sich die Aufführung als eine Hommage an Franz Kafkas gleichnamigen Roman mit gesellschaftskritischen Seitenhieben auf die damals auch medial sehr präsente, sogenannte Flüchtlingskrise. Der in dicke Winterjacken gehüllte Künstler kroch im wohl gepflegten Garten mühsam durch einen Tunnel aus Natodraht, fiesestem „Objektschutzdraht", zum Tor des Dätzinger Schlosses. Abschließend verband er die beiden Torflügel als lebendes, daran baumelndes Tür-Schloss und unterband so den Zugang zwischen Straße und Sekt-Ausschank (S. 16/17). Ob die edel gekleideten Galeristen und die an ihren Gläsern vornehm nippenden Stammbesucher die involvierte Gesellschaftskritik bemerkt haben, mag angezweifelt werden. Aber gerade das macht vielleicht die Qualität von Putzes Darbringungen aus! Dass sie oft nicht eindeutig zu lesen sind. Dass sie eine vermeintlich humorvolle, eine unterhaltende, aber eben auch eine tiefsinnige Seite haben. Man kann, muss aber die didaktischen Zwischentöne nicht erkennen. Der Künstler ist bei Thomas Putzes Darstellungen kein überheblicher, extrovertierter Paradiesvogel, sondern ein leidender, sich und die Friede-Freude-Eierkuchen-Welt in Frage stellender Zeitgenosse.

the laptops and sound devices of the musicians Günter Rolle and Michael Fiedler, who crafted together electronic live beats from it. To close the group show *Mitspieler* (Teammate) at Galerie Schlichtenmaier in Schloss Dätzingen in Grafenau, Putze had announced a performance entitled *Das Schloss* (The Castle, pp. 16/17). On site the performance revealed itself to be an homage to Franz Kafka's eponymous novel with its socio-critical dig at the so-called refugee crisis that was prevalent in the media of the time. In a well-tended garden and wrapped in a thick winter jacket, the artist arduously crawled through a course of razor-barbed wire—the nastiest possible "guard wire" used to protect objects—to the gate of Schloss Dätzingen. Once there he used himself to join together the two wings of the gate, becoming a living, dangling lock, thus preventing access between the street and the sparkling wine bar. Whether the well-dressed gallerists and the regular visitors genteelly sipping at their glasses noticed the social critique involved can only be doubted. But perhaps it is exactly that which constitutes the quality

„Warum einfach, wenn es auch schwer geht?", scheint das Motto von Thomas Putze und (teils) auch von mir zu sein. Mit der Messe-Koje meiner Stuttgarter Galerie *Schacher – Raum für Kunst* lote ich seit einigen Jahren auf der Art Karlsruhe die Grenzen des Dort-Machbaren aus. Dass die Karlsruher Kunstmesse nicht für Performances gedacht und geeignet ist, ist jedem klar: dem Veranstalter, dem Messe-Beirat, den Galeristen, den Besuchern und den Künstlern. Mir auch. Umso mehr Spaß macht es, die verstopften Köpfe der Aussteller und Besucher aus dem Stand-by-Bereich zu befreien und ihnen ein Lächeln zu schenken. Nachdem in den Jahren zuvor schon Jenny Winter-Stojanovic, Jürgen Oschwald und Jim Avignon temporäre Plastiken, Körperskulpturen und Aktionen darboten, verdeutlichte Thomas Putze im Februar 2020 unter dem Titel *Kraftakt II* die Schwierigkeit und buchstäbliche Schwere des Entstehungsprozesses künstlerischer Arbeiten. In einer Art Fitnessstudio, das zugleich Schauraum war, hat der in Sportklamotten steckende Künstler in und vor der Messe-Koje mittels selbstgebauter Sportgeräte Portraits der Besucher gezeichnet und gemalt. Wahrscheinlich war das gern

of what Putze has to offer! That often it is not clearly discernible. That the works have a presumed humorous, entertaining yet also profound side. The didactic nuances are able to, but do not have to, be perceived. With Thomas Putze's displays, the artist is not an arrogant, extrovert bird of paradise, but rather an ailing contemporary questioning himself and our rose-tinted world.

"Why make it easy when it can also be difficult?" seems to be Thomas Putze's motto, and (to some extent) mine too. With the stand for my Stuttgart gallery, Schacher—Raum for Kunst, at the trade fair Art Karlsruhe, I have been exploring, for several years now, the limits of what is feasible there. It's clear to everyone that this art fair is not designed nor is it suitable for performances: to the organizer, the fair's advisory board, the gallerists, the visitors, and the artists. To me too. It is all the more fun, then, to liberate the congested heads of the exhibitors and visitors from stand-by mode and give them something to smile about. Following on from Jenny Winter-Stojanovic, Jürgen Oschwald, and Jim Avignon, who presented temporary sculptures, body sculptures, and actions in previous years, Thomas Putze illustrated the difficulty and literal

bei Vernissagenreden eingesetzte Zitat von Karl Valentin „Kunst ist schön, macht aber viel Arbeit“ noch nie so wahr, wie bei dieser Aktion. Durch selbst auferlegte Handicaps in Form von anzuhebenden Gewichten erschwerte sich Thomas Putze den Arbeitsprozess kolossal. Die hohe körperliche Anstrengung führte dazu, dass die beim Fingerhakeln gegen ein 30 Kilo-Gewicht und mittels Roll-Hantel oder auf dem Hometrainer mit einer langen Eisenstange gezeichneten Portraits in nur wenigen Minuten, teils auch Sekunden abgeschlossen sein mussten. Dass die Bilder dennoch – oder wegen des (Zeit-)Drucks gerade deswegen? – mit einem großen Wiedererkennungswert aufwarteten, erstaunte viele. Klar, dass Thomas Putze auch eine mit Pinsel ausstaffierte Gitarre als Utensil einsetzte, nebenher Country-Songs spielte und sang und das „Feld“ zwischenzeitlich ihn besuchenden Familienangehörigen und neu gewonnenen Freundinnen und Freunden überließ, die gern in die von allen neugierig beäugte Künstler-Rolle schlüpften. Wobei es diese „Rolle“ eigentlich gar nicht gab und gibt. Okay, Thomas Putze wagt oft ein wenig mehr, als wir wagen. Er plant ein mögliches Scheitern mit ein und sieht vermeintlichen Fehlern gelassen entgegen. Auch im Nachhinein. Nichts ist perfekt. Nichts muss perfekt sein. So ist das Leben. Darum mag ich Thomas Putze und seine Kunst.

weight of the artistic creative process in February 2020, under the title *Kraftakt II* (Act of Strength II). In a type of fitness studio, which was also a display space, the artist, dressed in sports gear, drew and painted portraits of the visitors in and at the stand with the aid of sports equipment he had constructed himself. The quote by Karl Valentin readily used in vernissage speeches that “art is beautiful, but it takes a lot of work” has likely never been more true than with this action. Thomas Putze impeded his working process massively by self-inflicted handicaps in the form of weights. The enormous physical effort compelled him to finish drawing the portraits—which were created with his fingers wrestling against a 30-kilogram weight and by means of a barbell or on the exercise machine with a long iron bar—in just a few minutes, sometimes even seconds. Many were amazed that that the pictures nevertheless—or, due to the (time) pressure, because of?—came up with a good likeness. Of course, Thomas Putze also used a tool made from a guitar equipped with a brush and played and sang Country songs while relinquishing his “domain” to visiting family members and newly gained friends—who happily slipped into the role of the artist—whom everyone was watching with interest. Yet this “role” did not and does not actually exist. Okay, Thomas Putze is often a little more daring than we are. He plans for potential failure and looks on would-be mistakes with equanimity. Also in hindsight. Nothing is perfect. Nothing has to be perfect. Such is life. That is why I like Thomas Putze and his art.

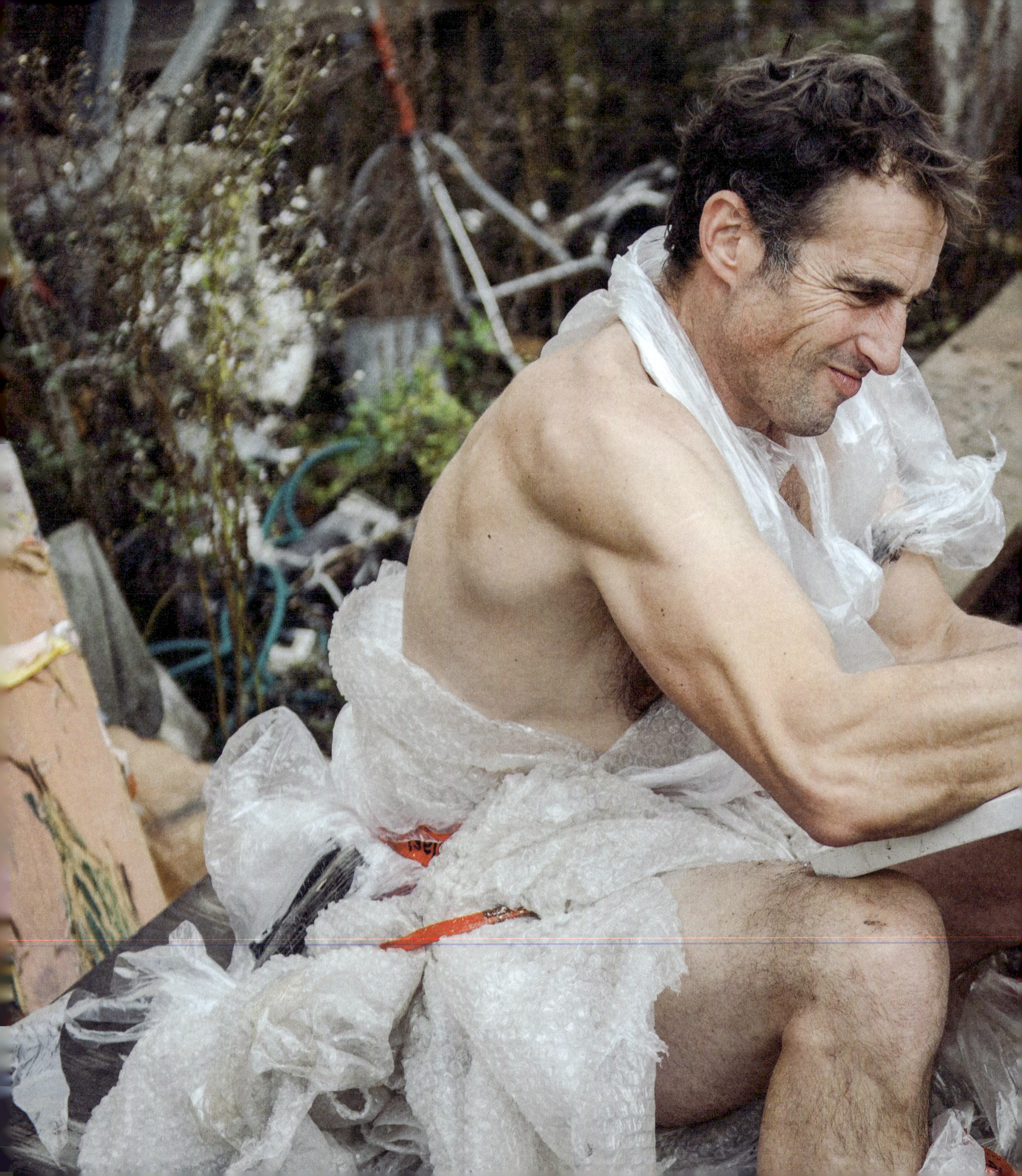

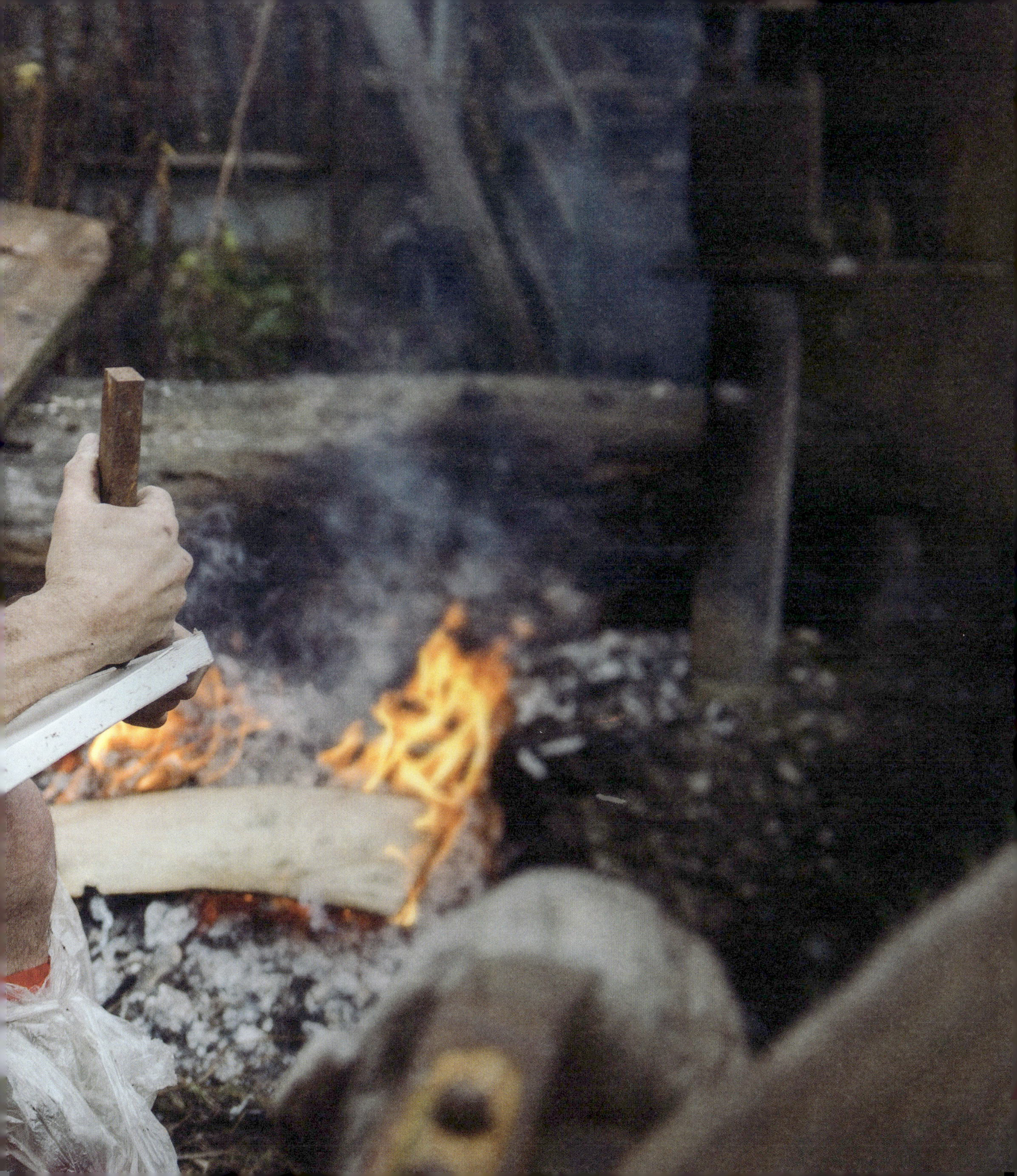

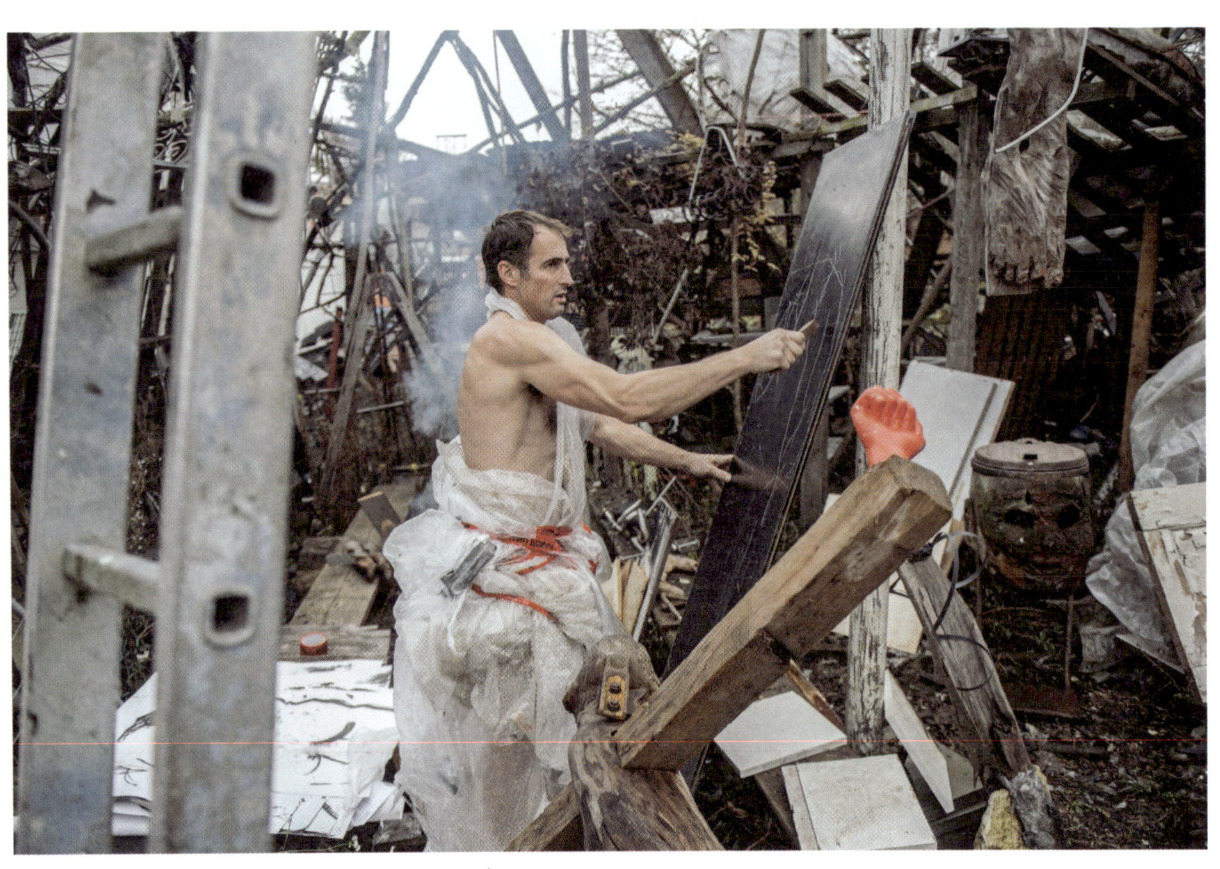

Mai / May 2019

Kraftakt I

Performance und Ausstellung im Auftrag von KISS e.V., Koordinationsstelle der Selbsthilfegruppen Stuttgart. Unter enormer körperlicher Anstrengung, über Kopf hängend, mit Gewichten belastet, flexend, zeichnend oder sägend, porträtierte der Künstler in seinem Atelier in Stuttgart Mitglieder diverser Selbsthilfegruppen. Jenen Kraftakt, den die Menschen vollbringen, wenn sie sich ihren Problemen stellen, übertrug er dabei sinnbildlich auf sich und sein künstlerisches Tun. Aufgrund der großen Anstrengung mussten die Porträts in nur wenigen Minuten entstehen.
Die Porträts von außerordentlicher Intensität wurden in einer Ausstellung im Stuttgarter Rathaus vom 14. Mai bis 6. Juni 2019 gezeigt.
Die Performance setzte der Künstler mit *Kraftakt II* während der Art Karlsruhe im Februar 2020 mit selbstgebauten Fitnesszeichengeräten fort (S. 8/9).

Performance and exhibition of behalf of KISS e.V., the information center and point of contact for support groups in Stuttgart. Hanging upside down in his Stuttgart studio, laden with weights and under immense physical strain while flexing, drawing, or sawing, the artist created portraits of members of various support groups. He symbolically transferred their acts of strength in facing up to their problems to himself and his artistic action. Due to the great effort involved, the portraits had to be created in just a few minutes.
These extraordinarily intense portraits were displayed in an exhibition at Stuttgart City Hall from May 14 to June 6, 2019. The artist continued the performance using his homemade sports equipment with *Kraftakt II* (Act of Strength II) during Art Karlsruhe, February 2020 (pp. 8/9).

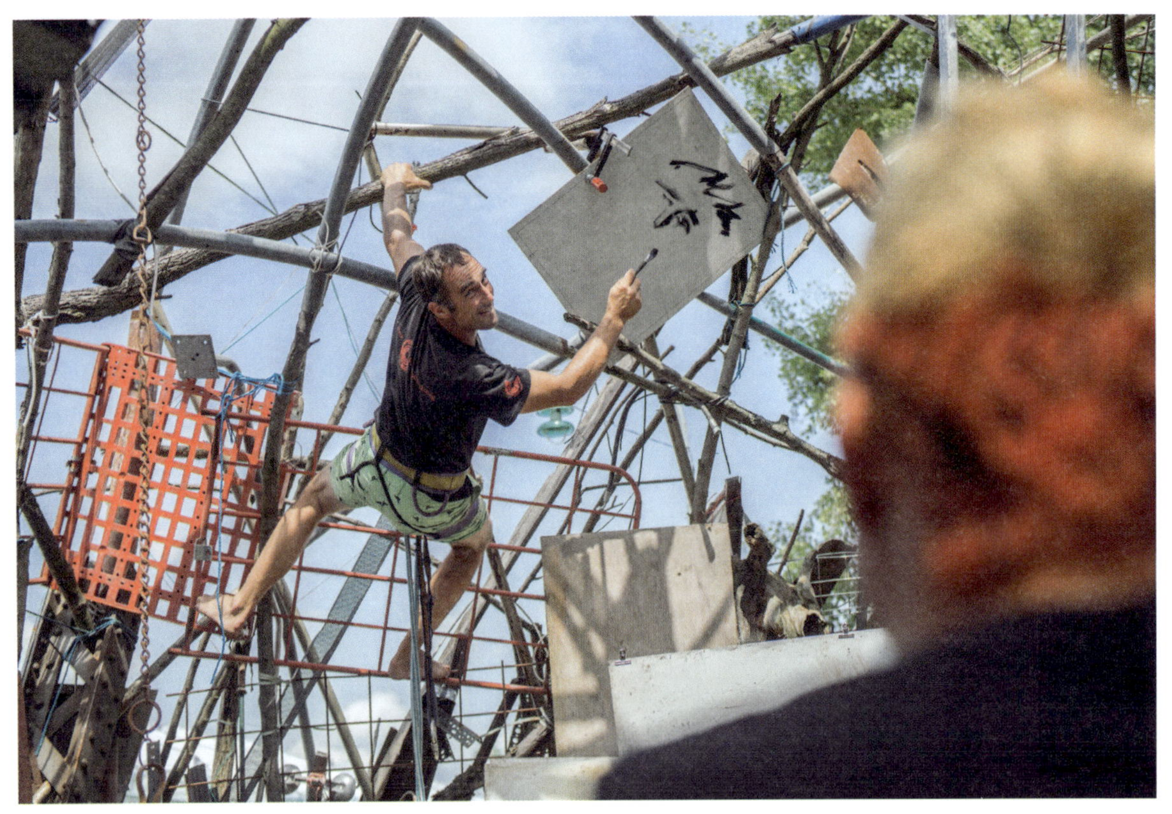

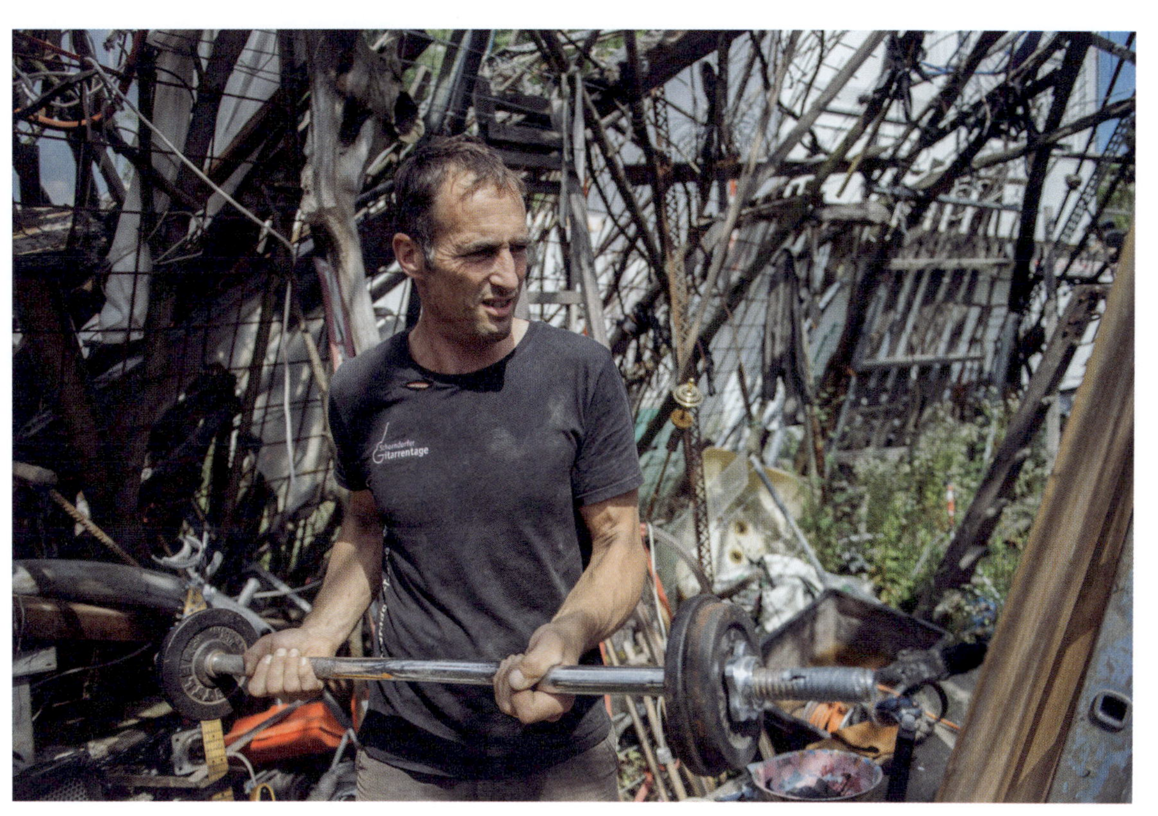
Schorndorfer
Gitarrentage

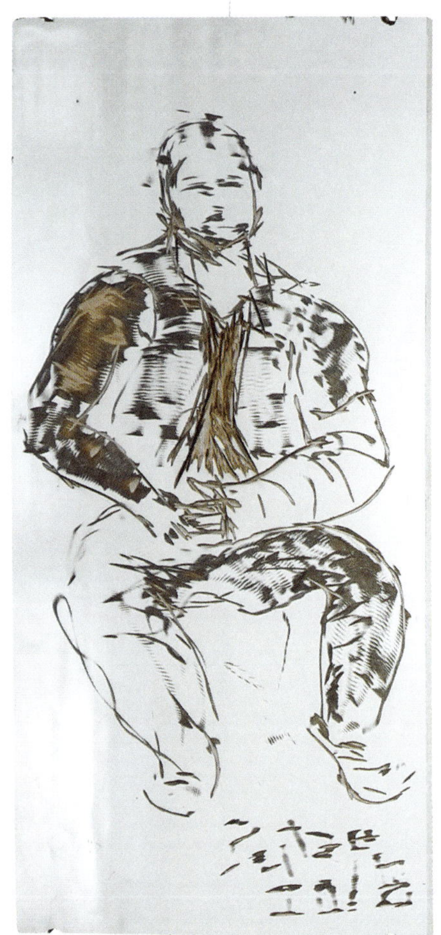

Die bei der *Kraftakt*-Performance entstandenen Porträts demonstrieren eindrucksvoll, mit welcher Geschwindigkeit und Präzision es dem Künstler gelang, die Wesensmerkmale unter den schwierigen Bedingungen zu erfassen.
The portraits created during the *Kraftakt* (Act of Strength) performance are an impressive demonstration of the speed and precision required by the artist to capture essential characteristics under the challenging conditions.

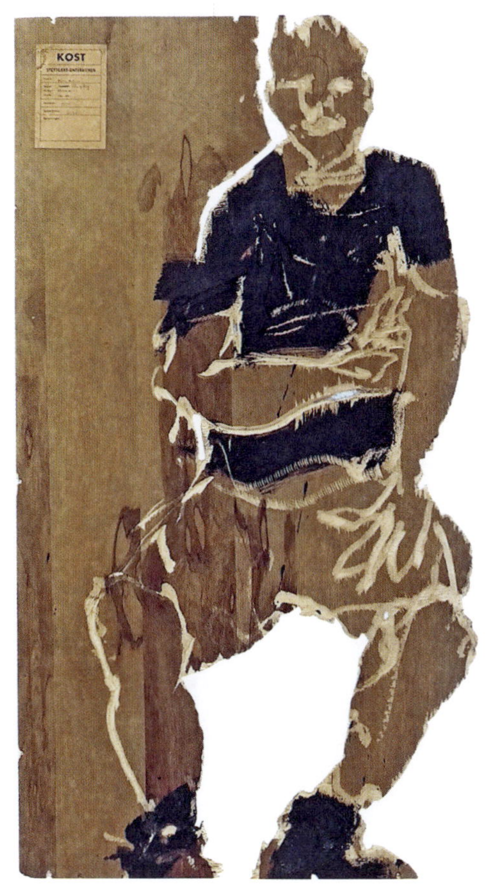
KOST

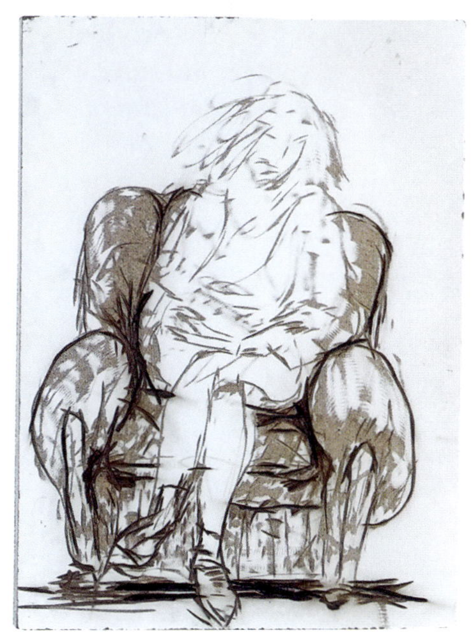

Juni /
June
2002

Klettern auf Solitude

Horizontale Kletteraktion auf dem Pflastersteinboden vor Schloss Solitude, anlässlich der Gruppenausstellung *Niveau* der Klasse Micha Ullmann.
Horizontal climbing action over paved ground in front of Schloss Solitude to mark the group exhibition *Niveau* by the class of Micha Ullmann.

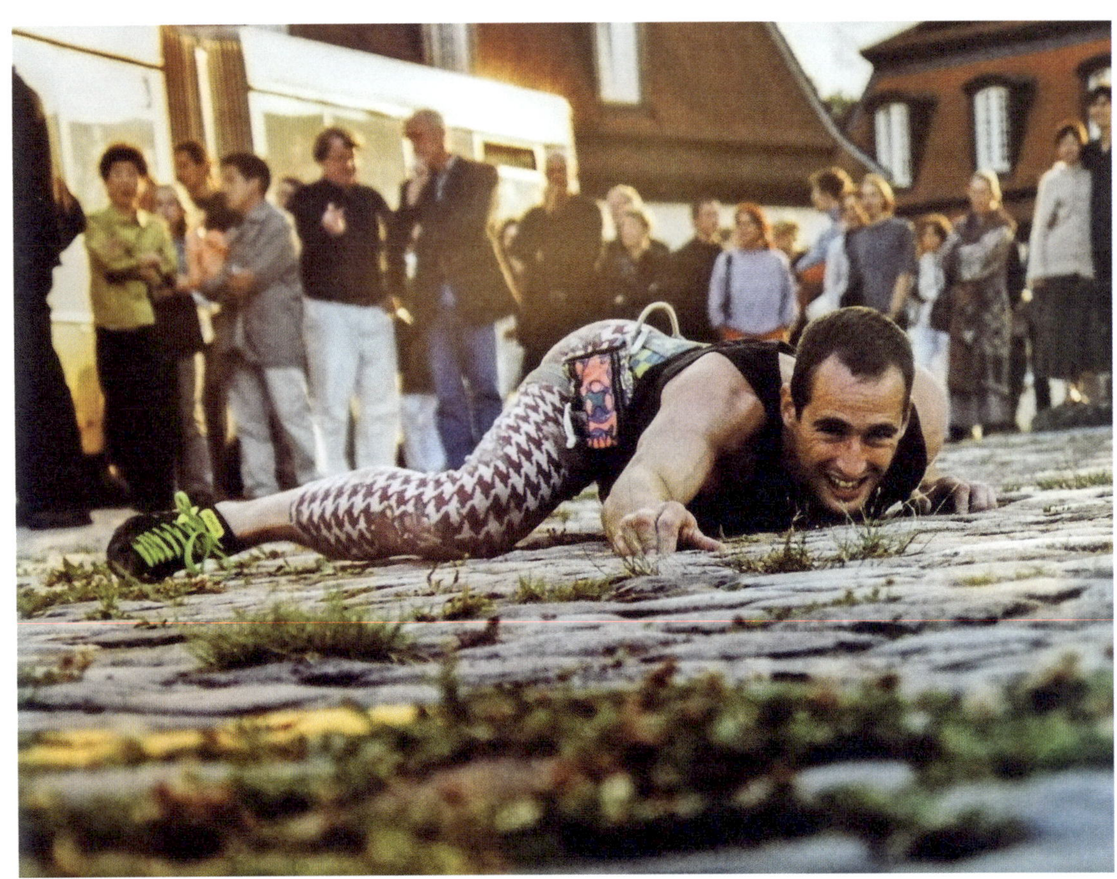

„[Thomas Putze begeht mit seinen Performances den] Weg eines Langstrecken-Kletterers, für den der Gipfel immer höher wird, immer schwerer zu erreichen. Wir steigen gemeinsam mit ihm, weil wir spüren, dass, je höher er kommt, desto tiefer findet er zu seiner eigenen Seele und wir dadurch auch zu unserer. Vielleicht ist sein Weg nicht weniger als der Kampf gegen die Gravitation, gegen die eigene Schwerkraft."
"[With his performances, Thomas Putze treads] the path of a long-distance climber for whom the summit is getting higher and higher, more and more difficult to reach. We climb with him for we feel that the higher he gets the deeper he finds his own soul, and with it ours too. Perhaps his path is nothing less than the struggle against gravitation, against his own gravity."

Micha Ullman

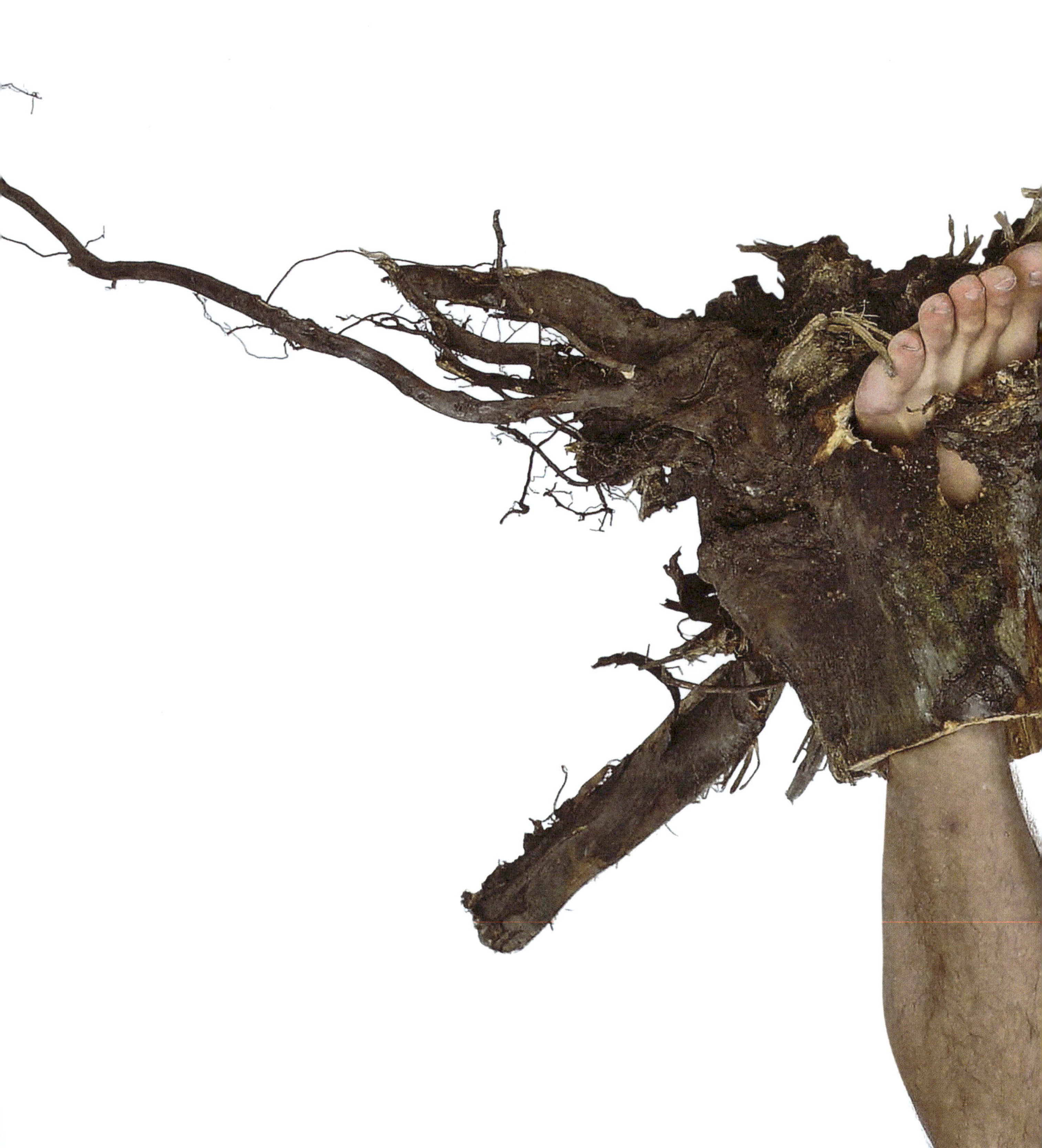

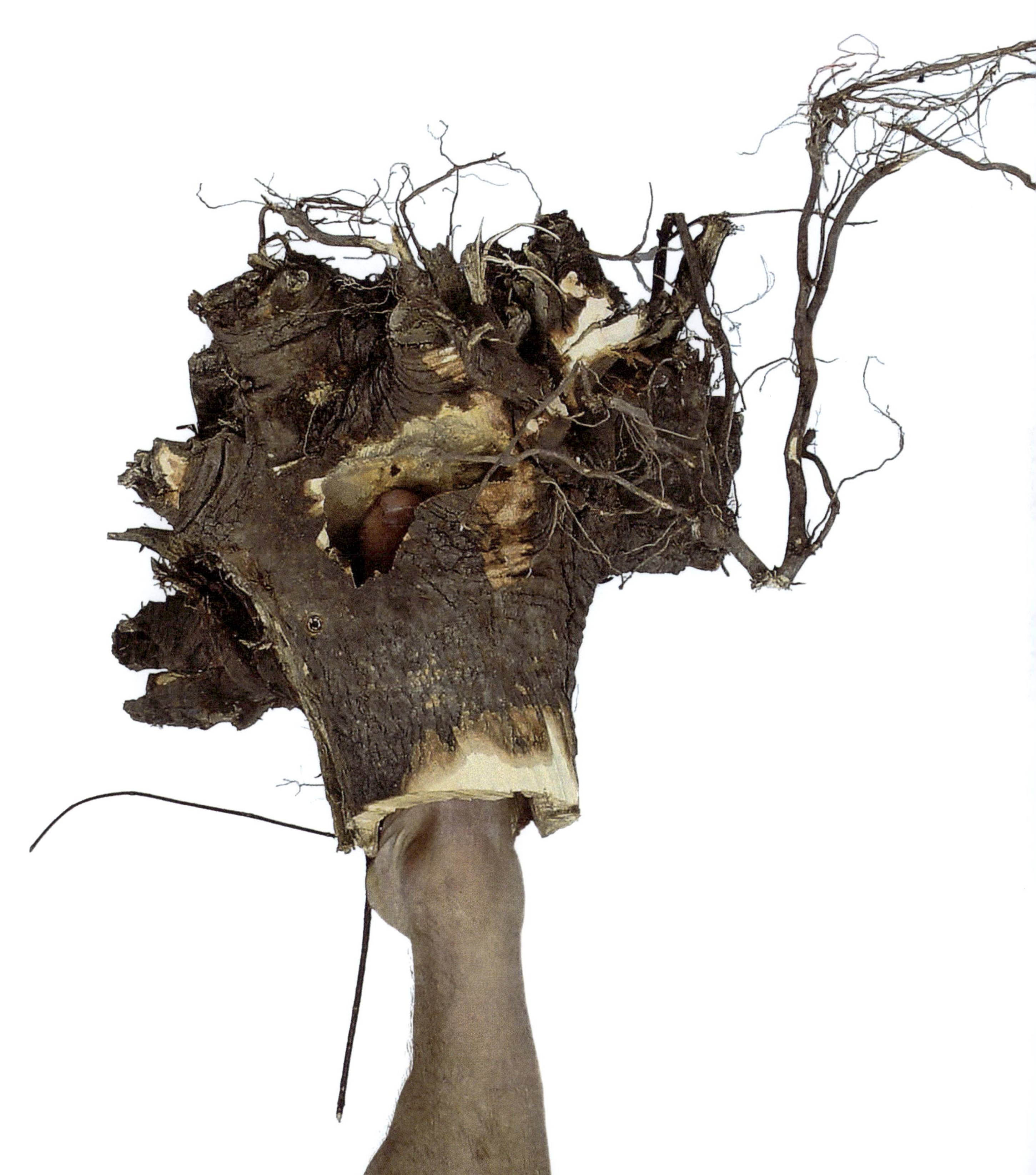

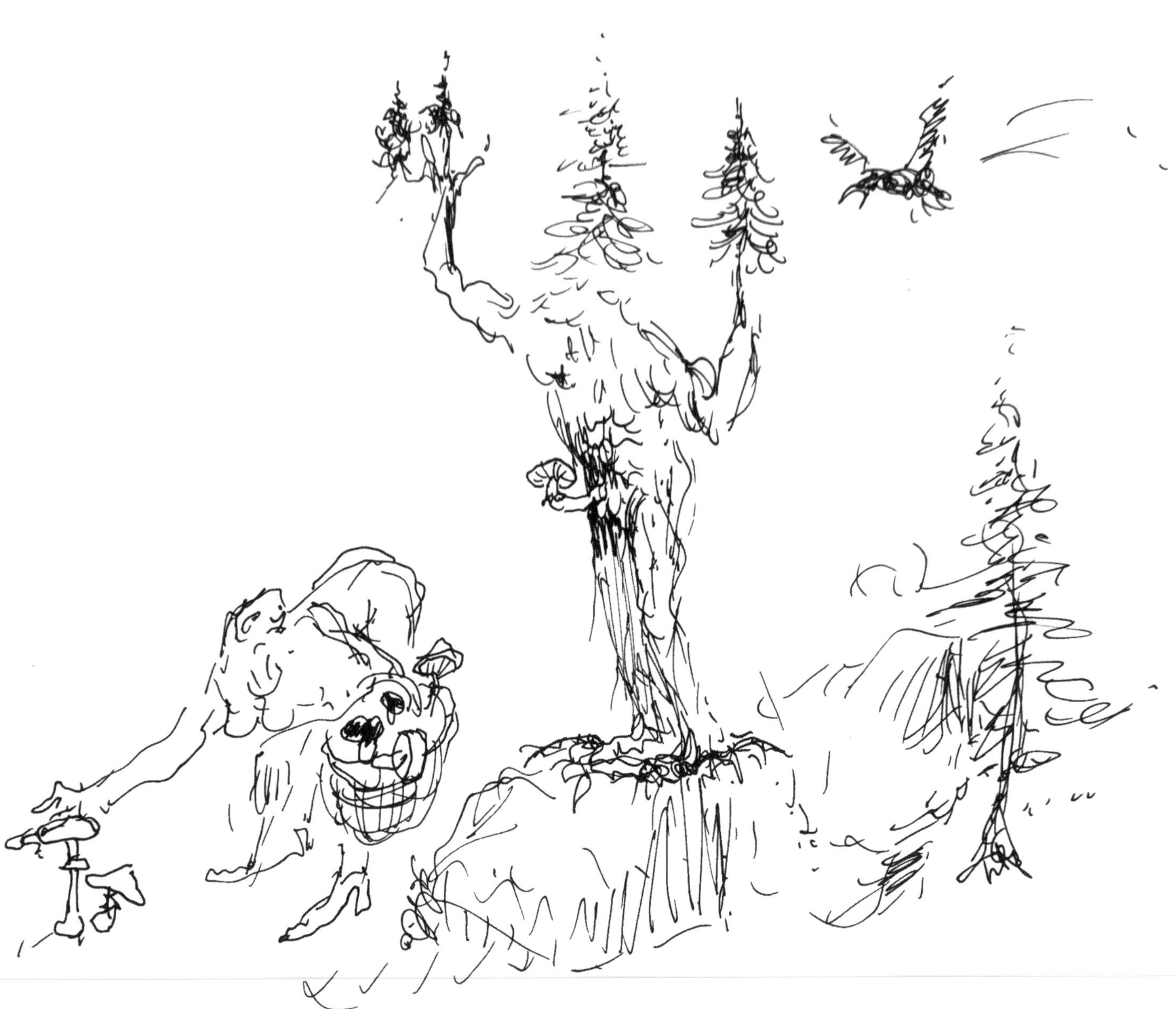

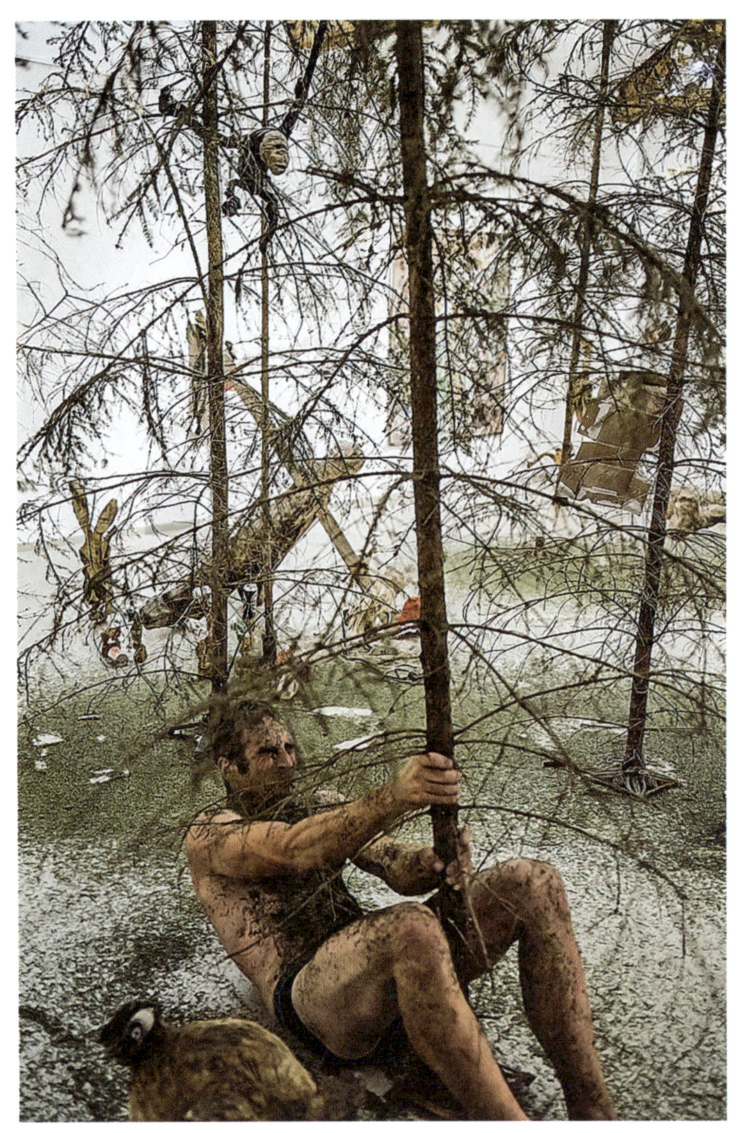

August 2018 — Nadelwald

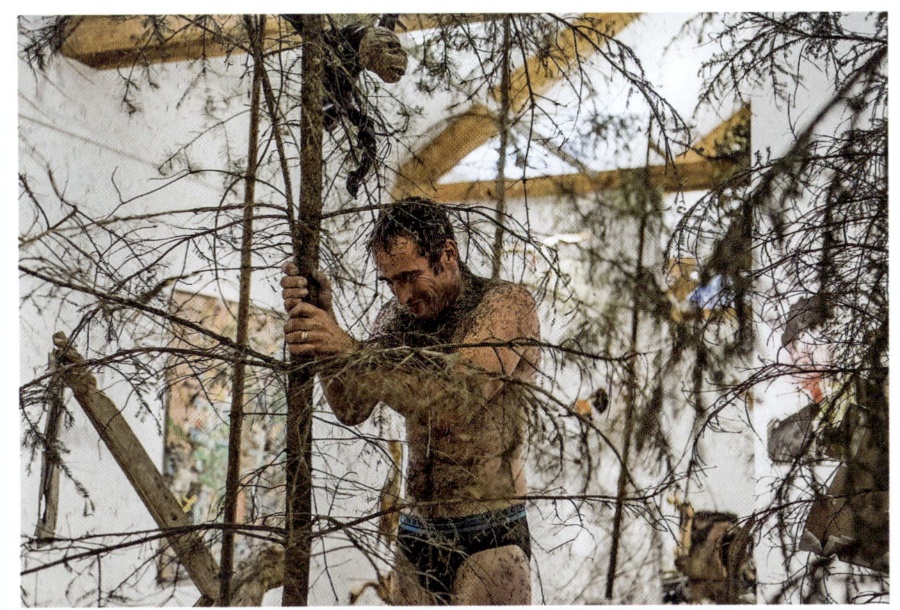

Performance zur Finissage der Gruppenausstellung *myths upcycled*, Kunststation Kleinsassen, am 17. August 2018. Der Künstler hinterließ mit dieser Performance seine Spuren in der Ausstellung und die Ausstellung hinterließ ihre Spuren auf ihm.
Performance for the closing day of the group exhibition *myths upcycled* at Kunststation Kleinsassen, August 17, 2018. Not only did the artist leave his mark on the exhibition with this performance; the exhibition also left its mark on him.

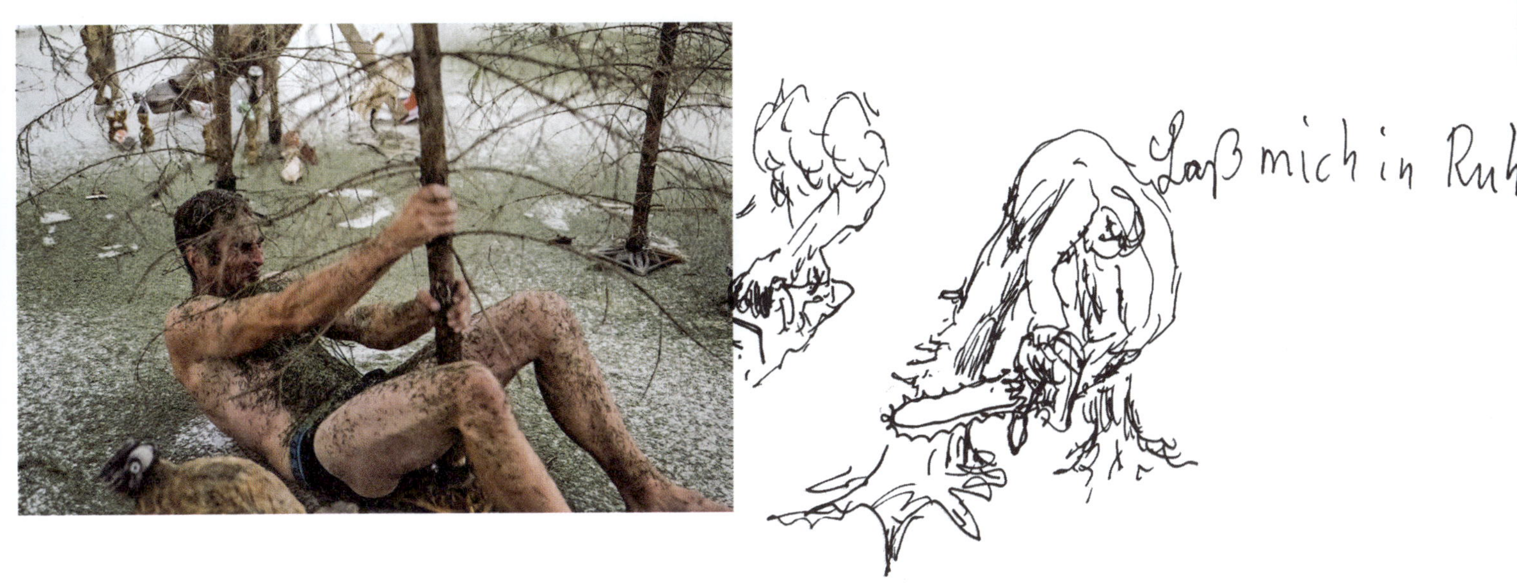

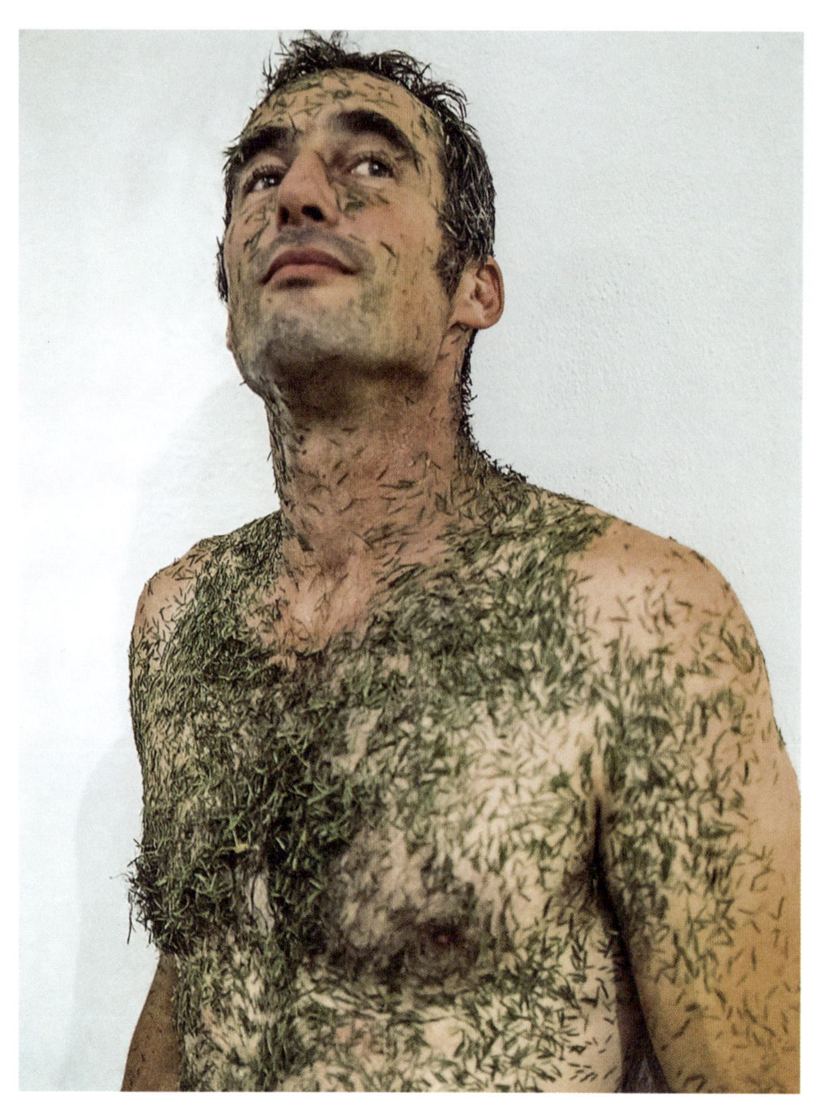

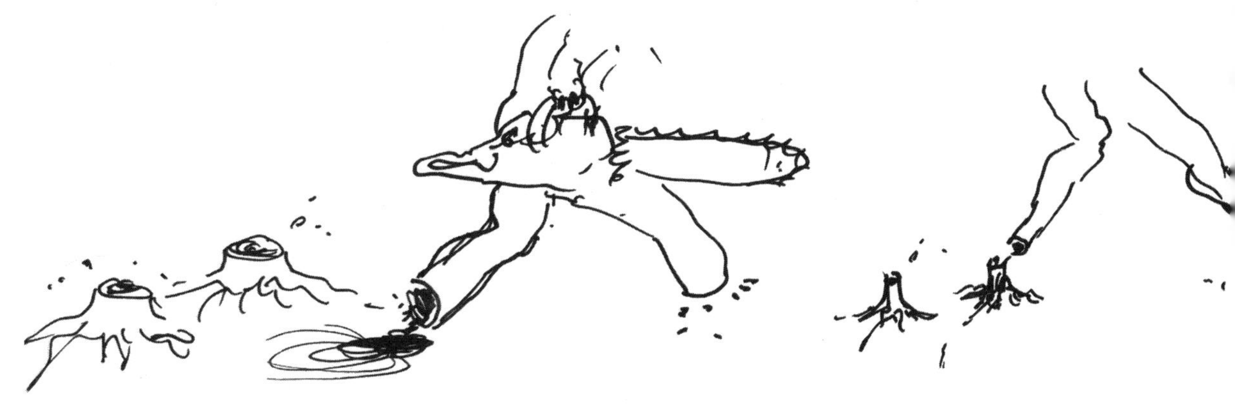

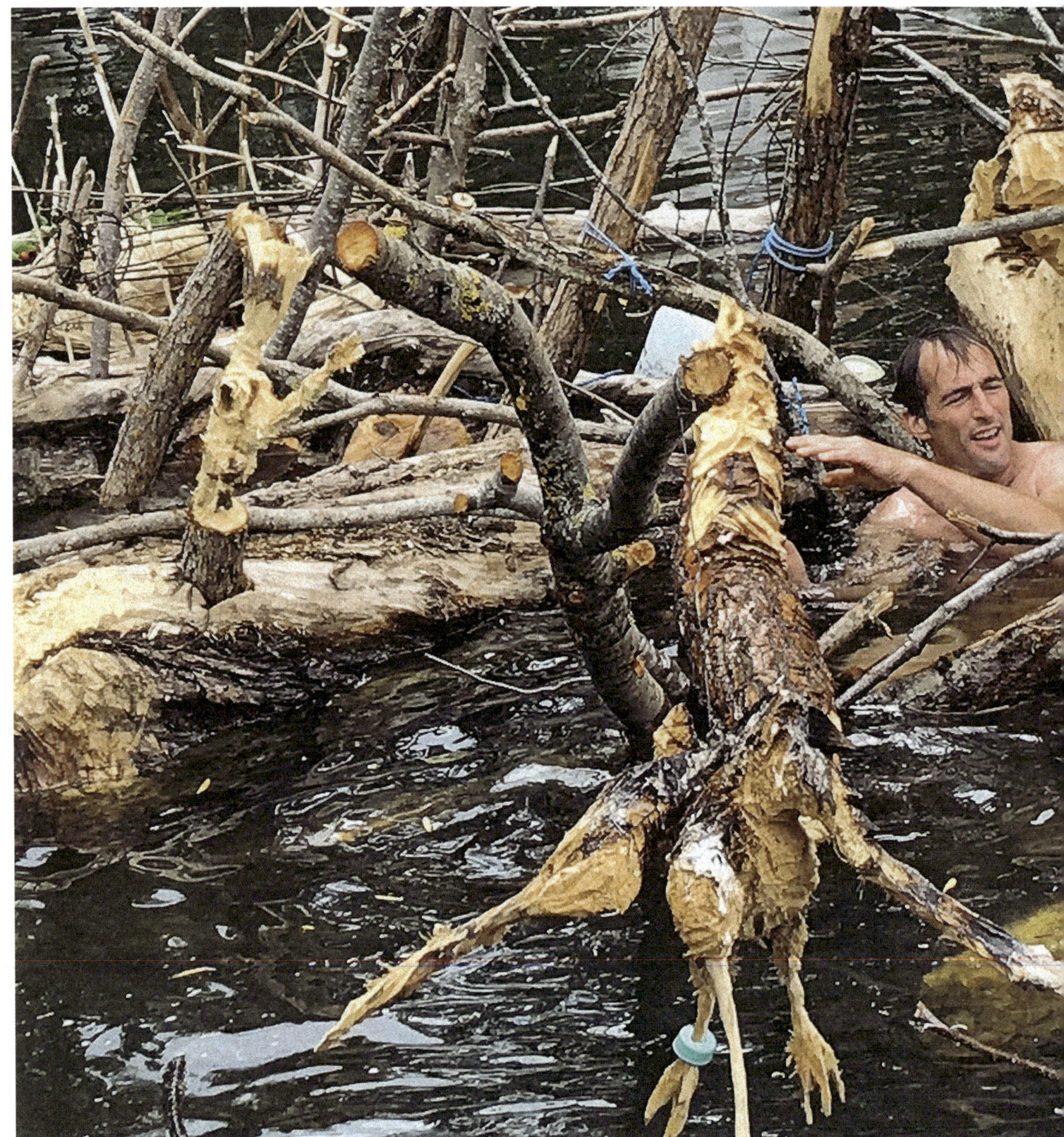

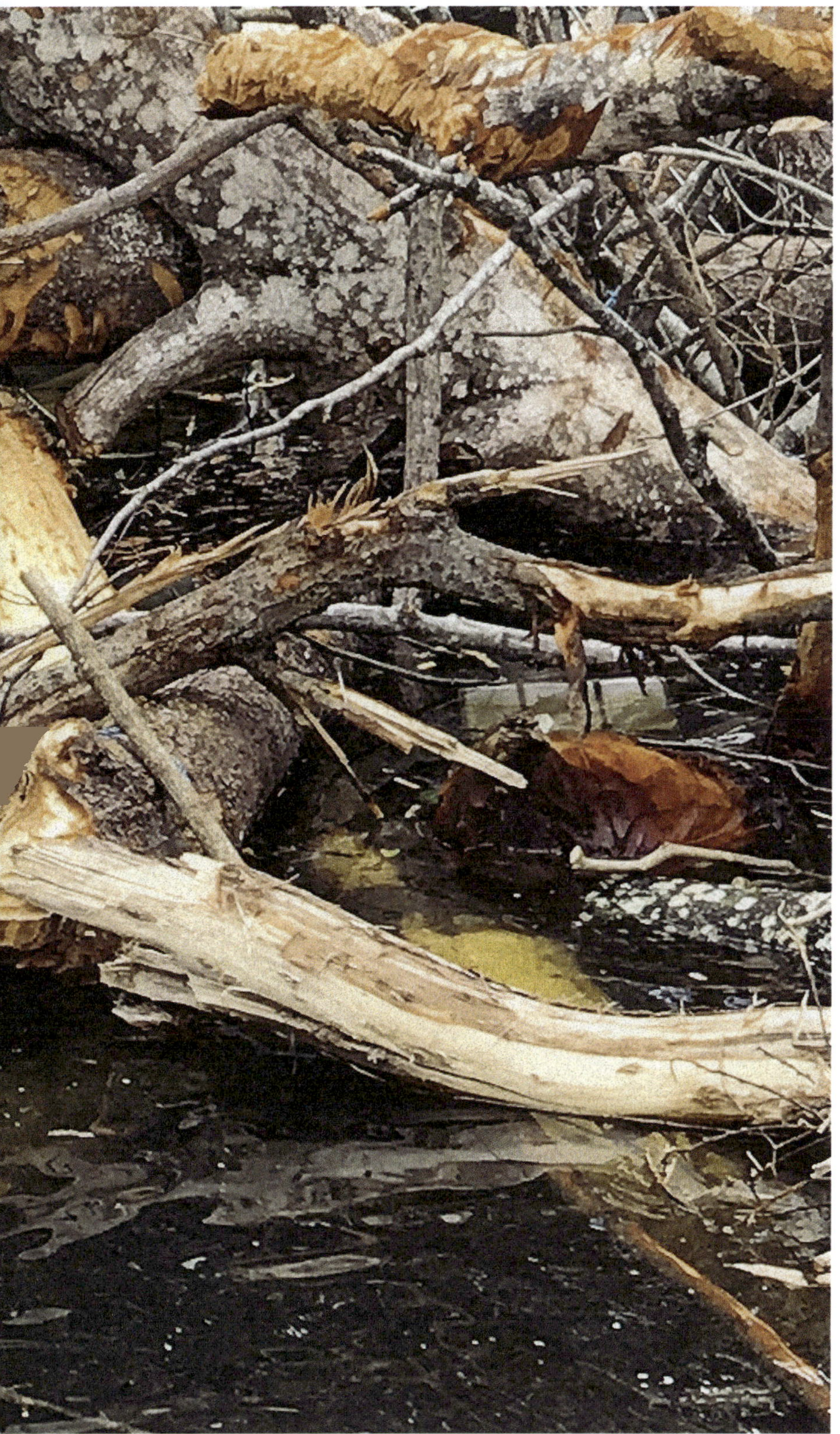

Juli / July 2019

Biber

Performance zur Eröffnung der Donaugalerie, ein Skulpturenprojekt der Stadt Tuttlingen, 14. Juli 2019. Der Biber als Holzbildhauer war dem Performancekünstler und Holzbildhauer Vorbild für die Installation *Biberbau* und die dazugehörige Performance. Diese begann mit einer Kletter- und Sägeaktion hoch oben in einer Weide am Ausstellungsgelände und endete mit dem schwimmenden Transport von Stämmen und Ästen zum Biberbau, durch den in die Rolle des Biber schlüpfenden Künstlers. Die Aufnahme zeigt Thomas Putze in seinem Element inmitten seiner Installation *Biberbau*.

Performance for the opening of the Donaugalerie, a sculpture project for the City of Tuttlingen, July 14, 2019. The performance artist and sculptor's model for the installation *Biberbau* (Beaver's Lodge) and its accompanying performance was the beaver as a sculptor of wood. This began with a climbing and sawing action high atop a willow tree at the exhibition grounds and ended with the floating transportation of tree trunks and branches for the lodge by the artist who had slipped into the role of a beaver. The photo shows Thomas Putze in his element surrounded by his Beaver's Lodge installation.

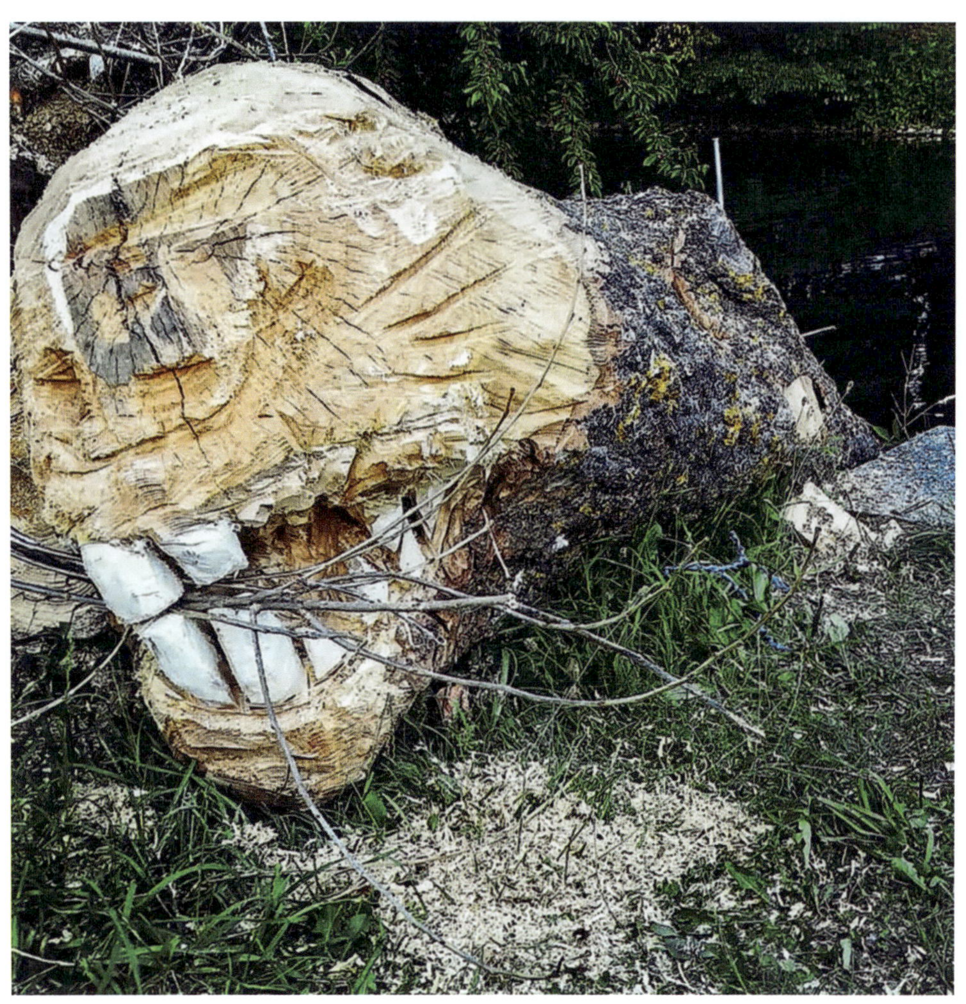

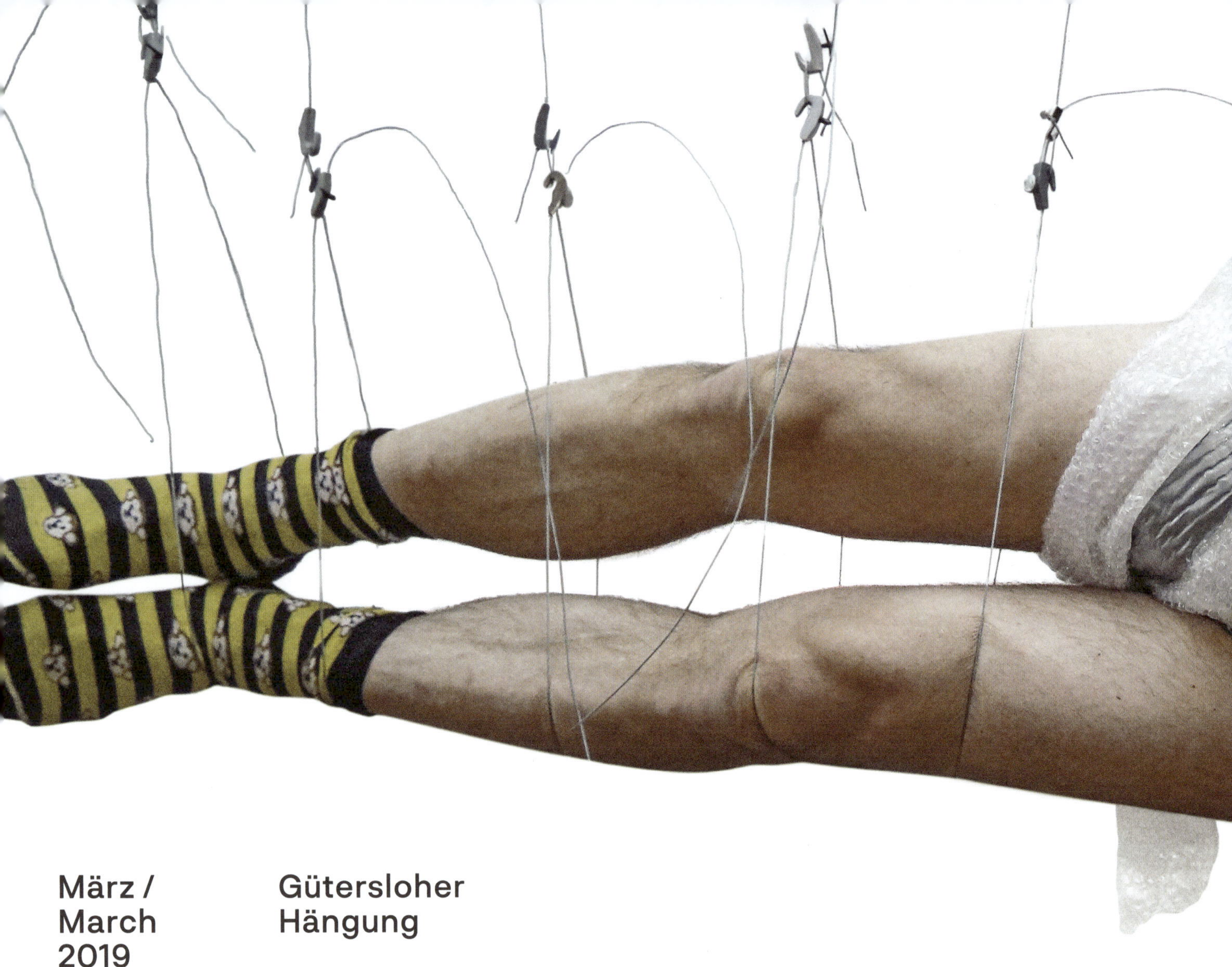

März /
March
2019

Gütersloher
Hängung

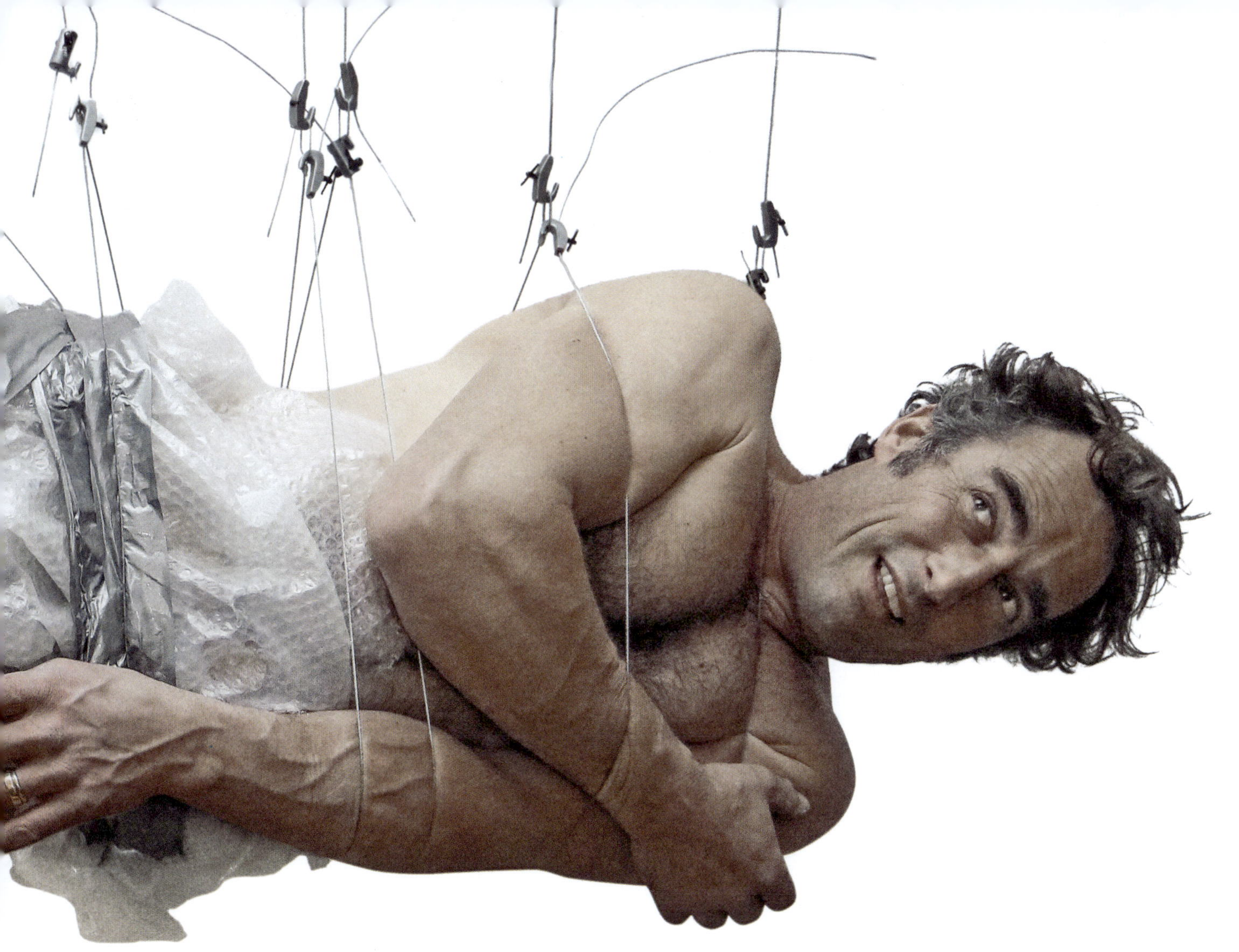

Performance am Galeriehängesystem zur Vernissage der Ausstellung *Thomas Putze außer sich*, Kunstverein Gütersloh, 3. März 2019.
Performance with the gallery's suspension system for the vernissage of the exhibition *Thomas Putze außer sich* (Thomas Putze beside Himself) at Kunstverein Gütersloh, March 3, 2019.

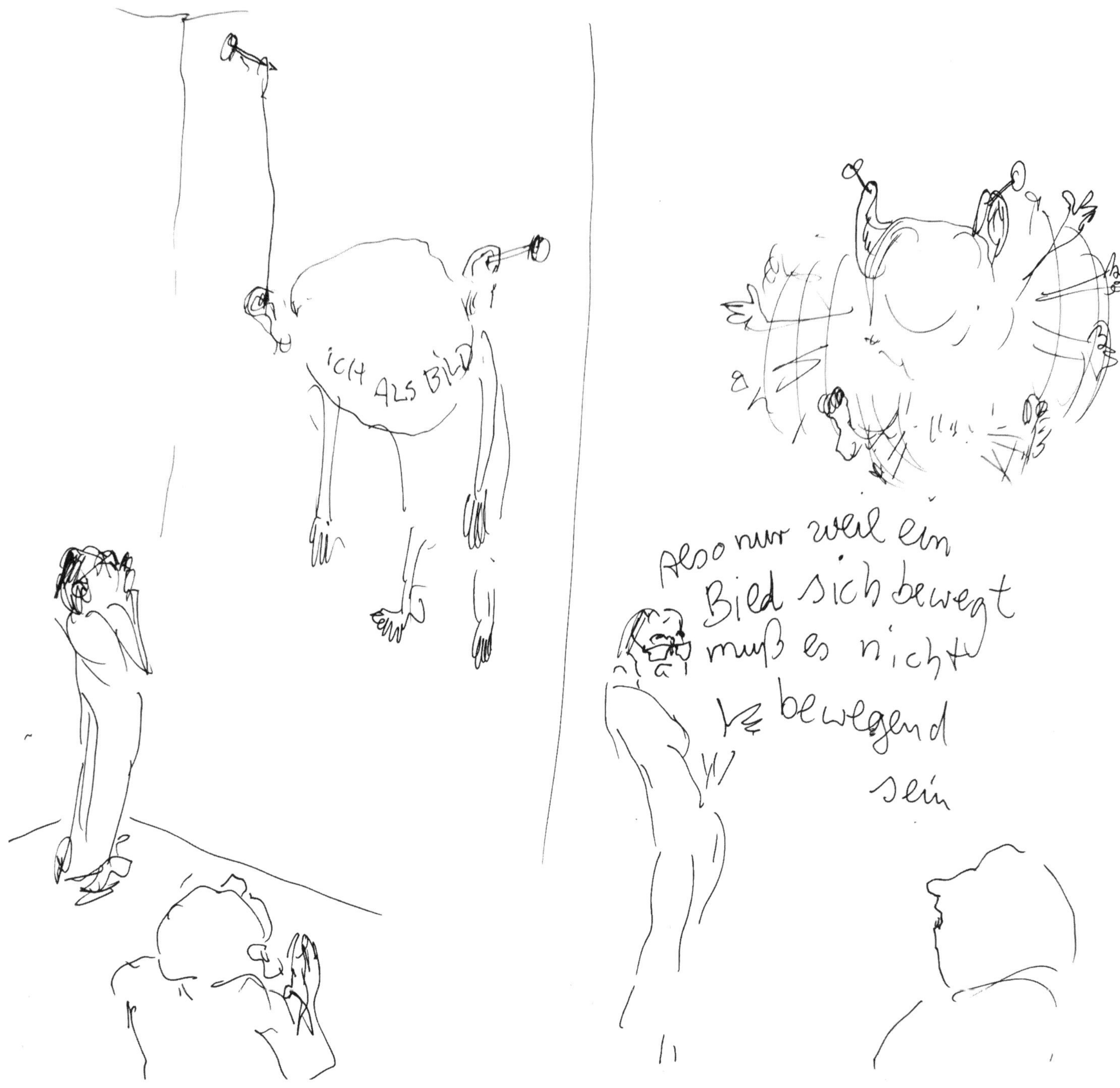
ICH ALS BILD
Also nur weil ein
Bild sich bewegt
muß es nicht
bewegend
sein

Er selbst scheint sich sehr erregend zu finden

regt mich sehr an

April 2019

Lange Leine

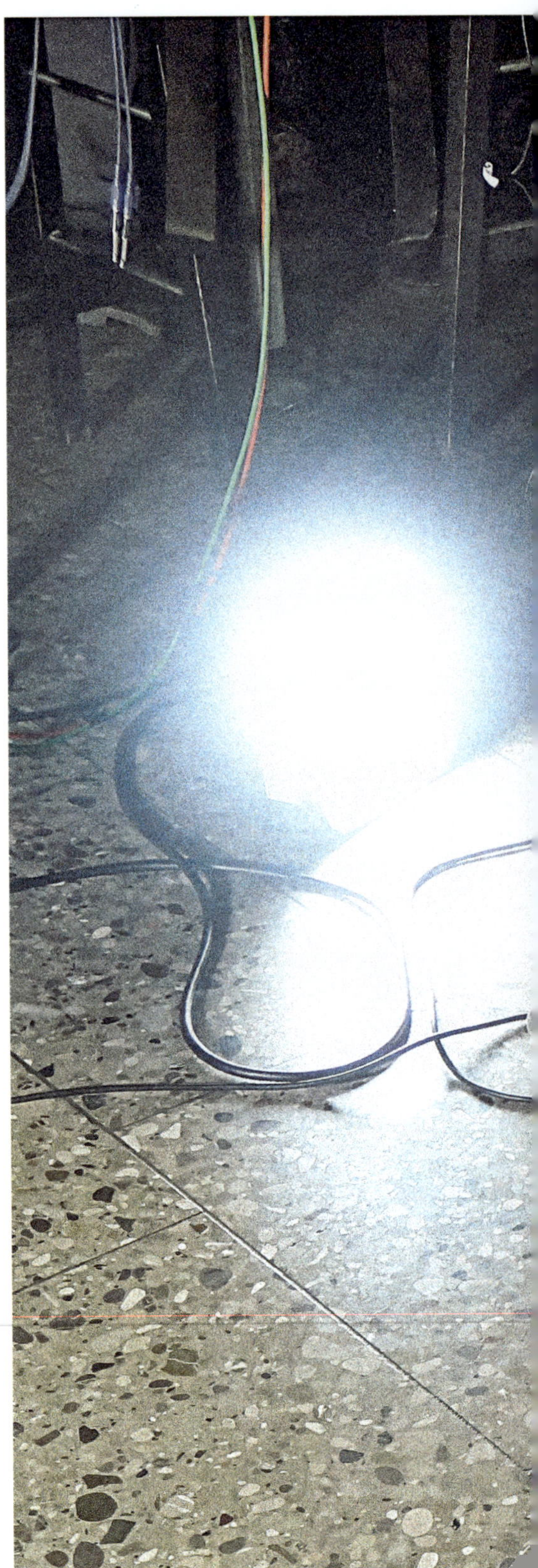

Klangperformance in Kooperation mit dem Musiker Duo Les Six, Michael Fiedler und Günter Rolle (†) im Theater Rampe, Stuttgart, am 15. April 2019. Sich aus dem Gewirr aus Elektrokabeln befreiend, durchklettert und ertastet der Künstler den Raum und sammelt durch an seinem Körper befestigte Mikrofone und Tonabnehmer verschiedenste Tonquellen. Durch die Bewegung wurden diese direkt über Kabel in das Mischpult der beiden Musiker gespeist und umgehend hörbar für die Zuschauer in eine musikalische Komposition verwandelt. Optische und akustische Impulse bedingten und steigerten sich und verwoben sich im Raum zu einer eigenen, dichten Realität.

Sound performance in collaboration with musical duo Les Six, Michael Fiedler and Günter Rolle (†), at Theater Rampe in Stuttgart, April 15, 2019. Unfettering himself from the entanglement of electric cables, the artist clambered and felt his way through the room, accumulating as he went the most diverse sounds through the microphones and pickups attached to his body. The sounds of his movements were fed directly via cable into the two musicians' mixing console and immediately converted into an audible musical composition for the onlookers. Optical and acoustic impulses were generated and boosted and interwove themselves in the space, forming their own consolidated reality.

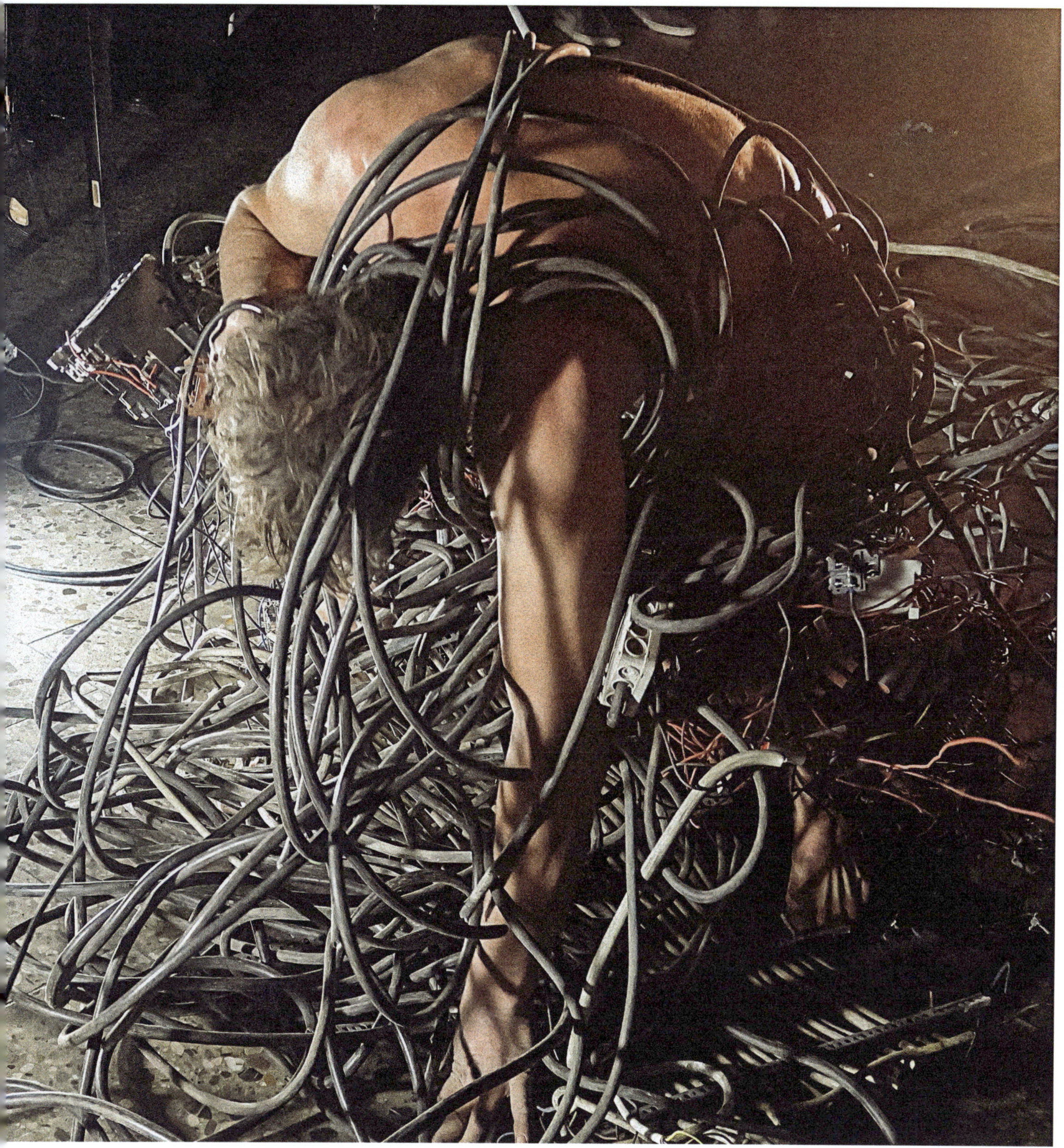

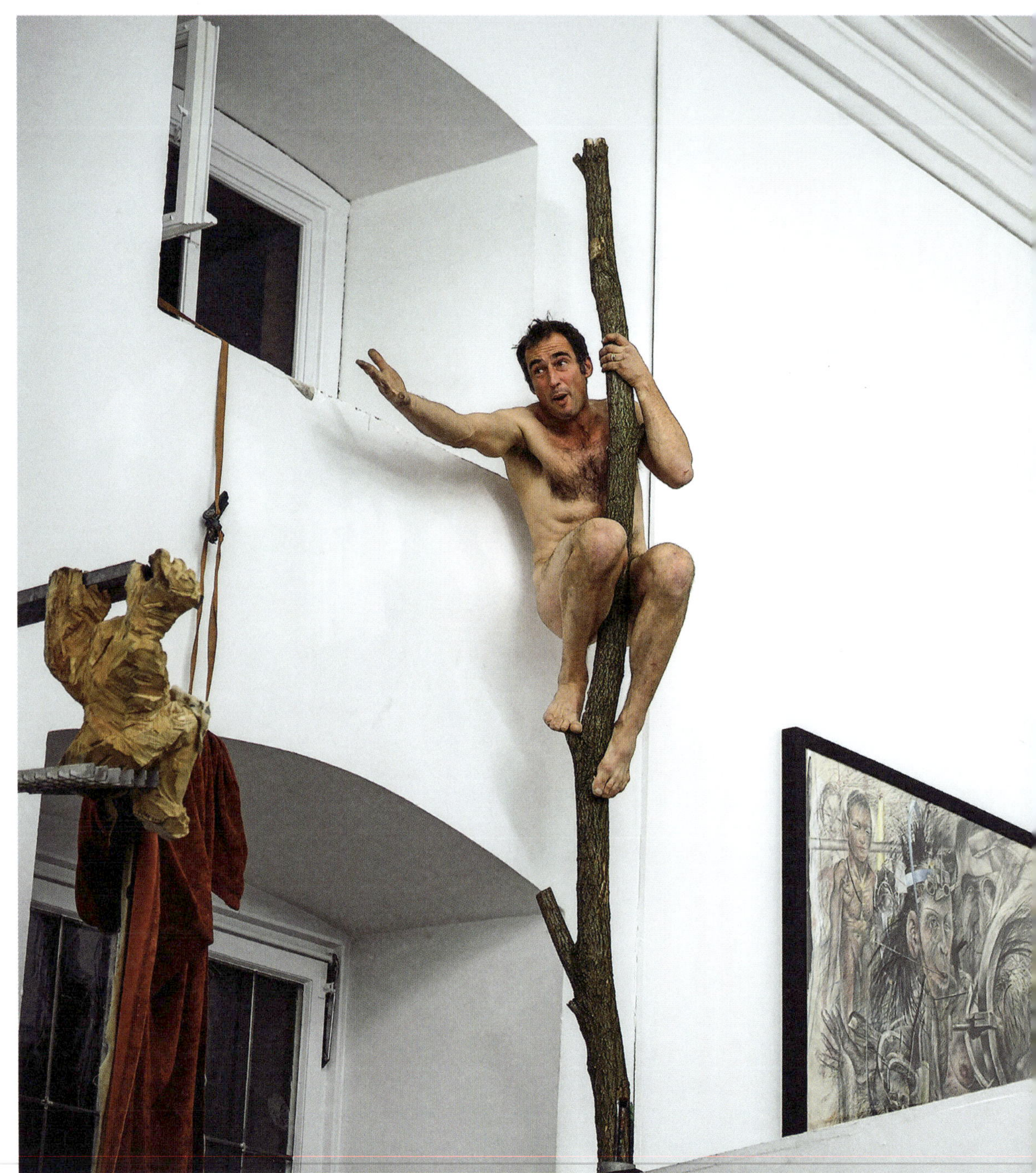

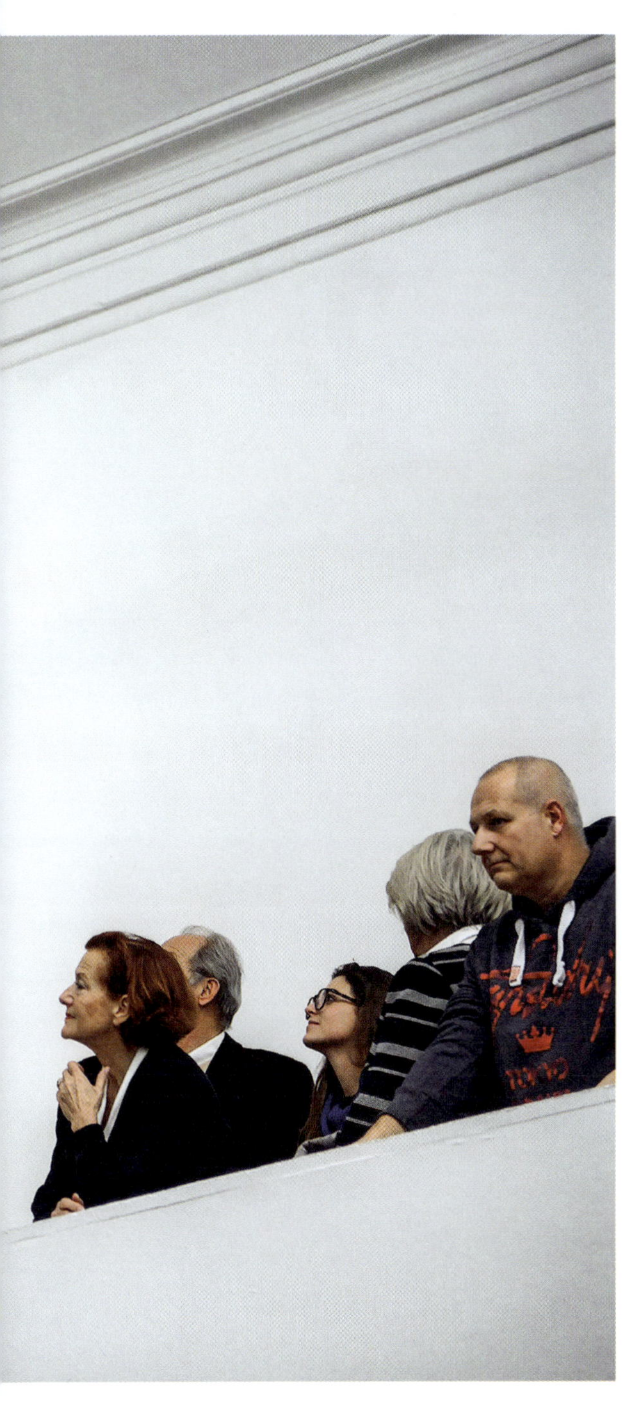

Performance zur Vernissage der gleichnamigen Ausstellung im Kunstforum Rottweil am 24. November 2018. Die wohl emblematischste Performance des Künstlers, der splitternackt aus einer Fensternische herab äffisch zuerst das Publikum und dann sich selbst beschimpfte und anbrüllte. Die Performance hinterfragt das eigene Tun als Künstler und Performer, der sich immer wieder zum Affen macht. Nach dem Warum fragend, kletterte der Künstler hinab ins Publikum, um sich dort mit Anzug, Turnschuhen und Sekt zurück zum Menschen zu verwandeln und unters Publikum zu mischen.
Performance for the vernissage of the eponymous exhibition in Kunstforum Rottweil, November 24, 2018. Probably the artist's most emblematic performance, in which he descended, naked and apishly, from a window recess before insulting and bawling at the audience. The performance questioned his own action as a performer and artist, one who repeatedly makes a monkey of himself. After questioning why, the artist entered the throng to then transform back into a human in a suit and sneakers with a sparkling wine and mix among the crowd.

November 2018

Affentheater

September 2019

Pendel

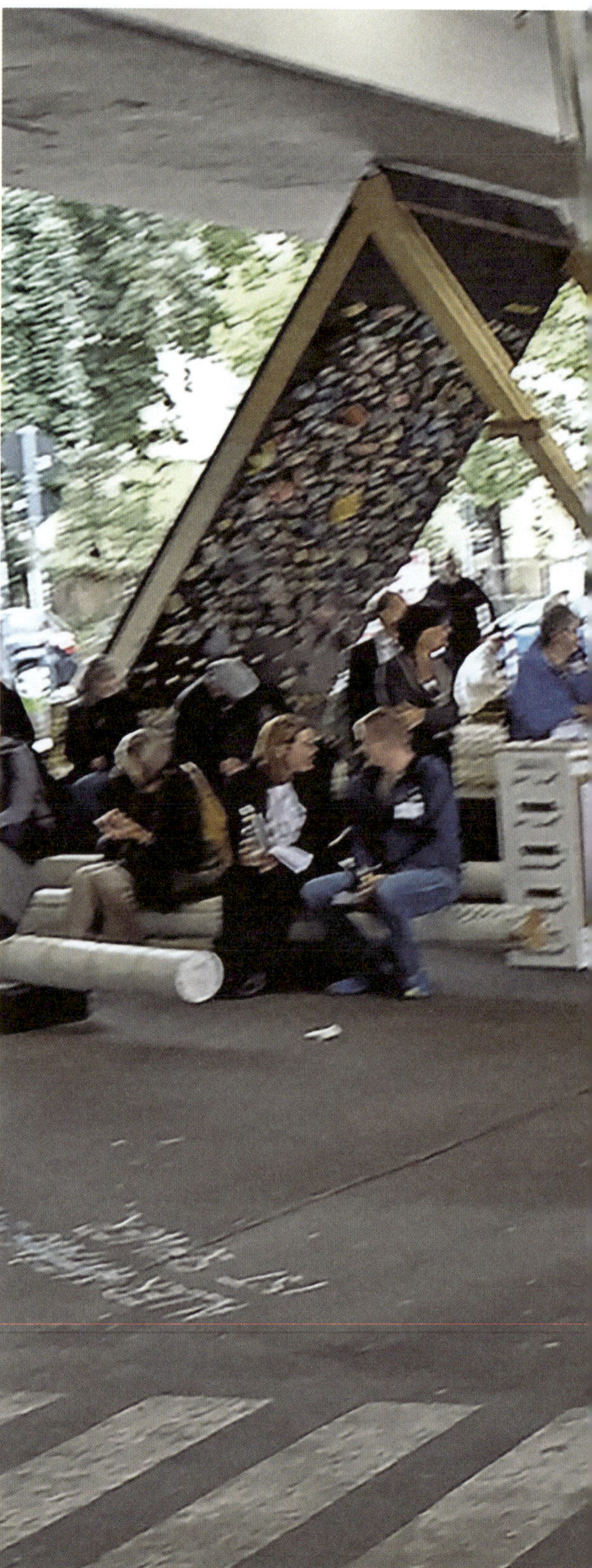

Performance mit Leinentuch und Metallplatte. *Pendel* fand im Kontext der Charta Initiative „Leben bis zum Schluss“ unter der Paulinenbrücke in Stuttgart statt. Das symbolische Leintuch, vom ersten Gewand bis zum Sterbehemd, war die Grundlage des Künstlers, der ansonsten unbekleidet und schutzlos gegen eine riesige Metallplatte schwang, gleich dem Leben als Pendelbewegung.

Performance with sheet and metal panel. *Pendel* (Pendulum) took place beneath the Paulinenbrücke (Pauline Bridge) in Stuttgart within the context of the Charta initiative "Leben bis zum Schluss" (Live to the End). The symbolic sheet—from first garment to funeral gown—was the basic concept for the artist, who without clothes himself and with no protection swung against a giant metal panel, akin to life as a pendulum in motion.

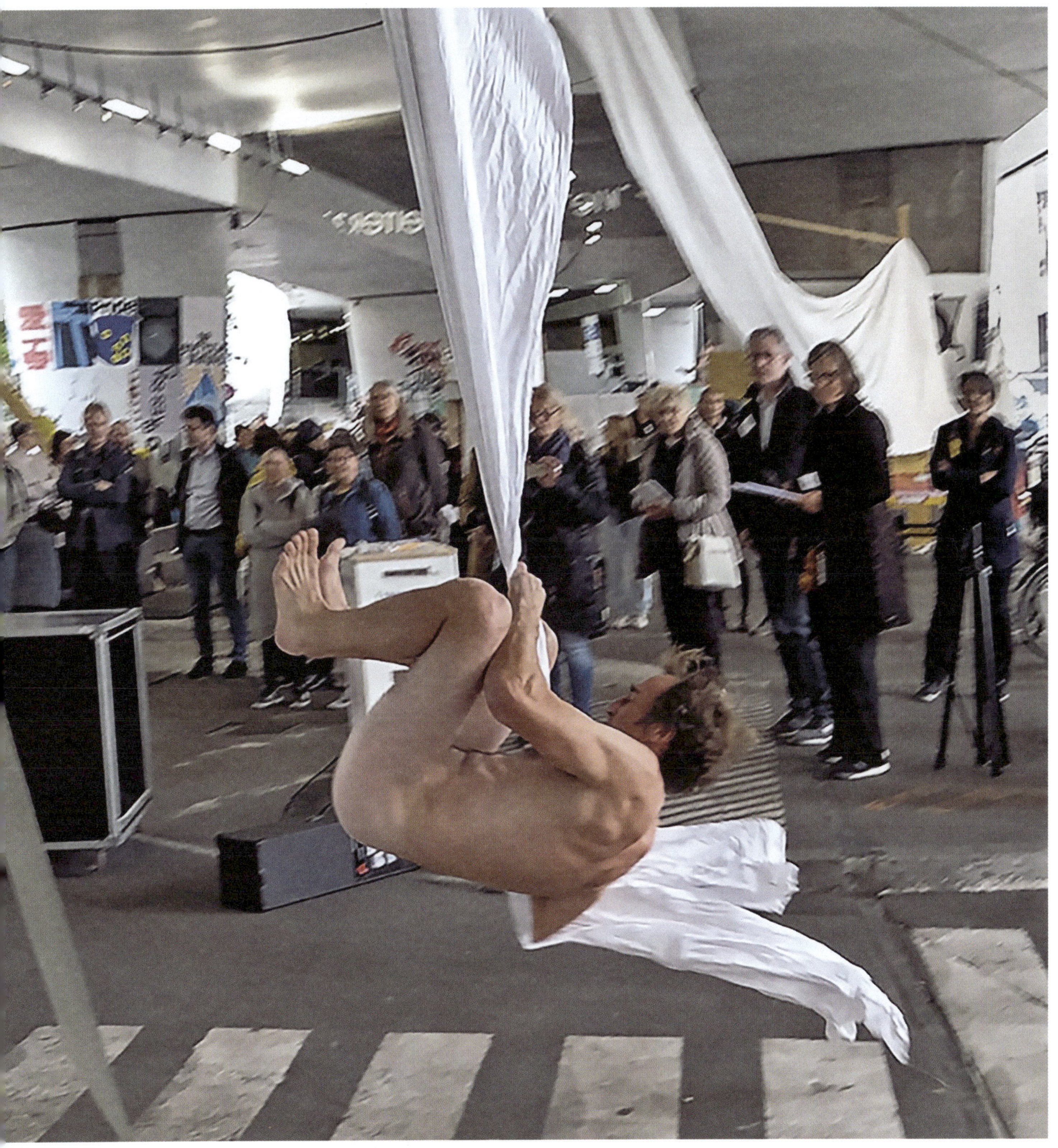

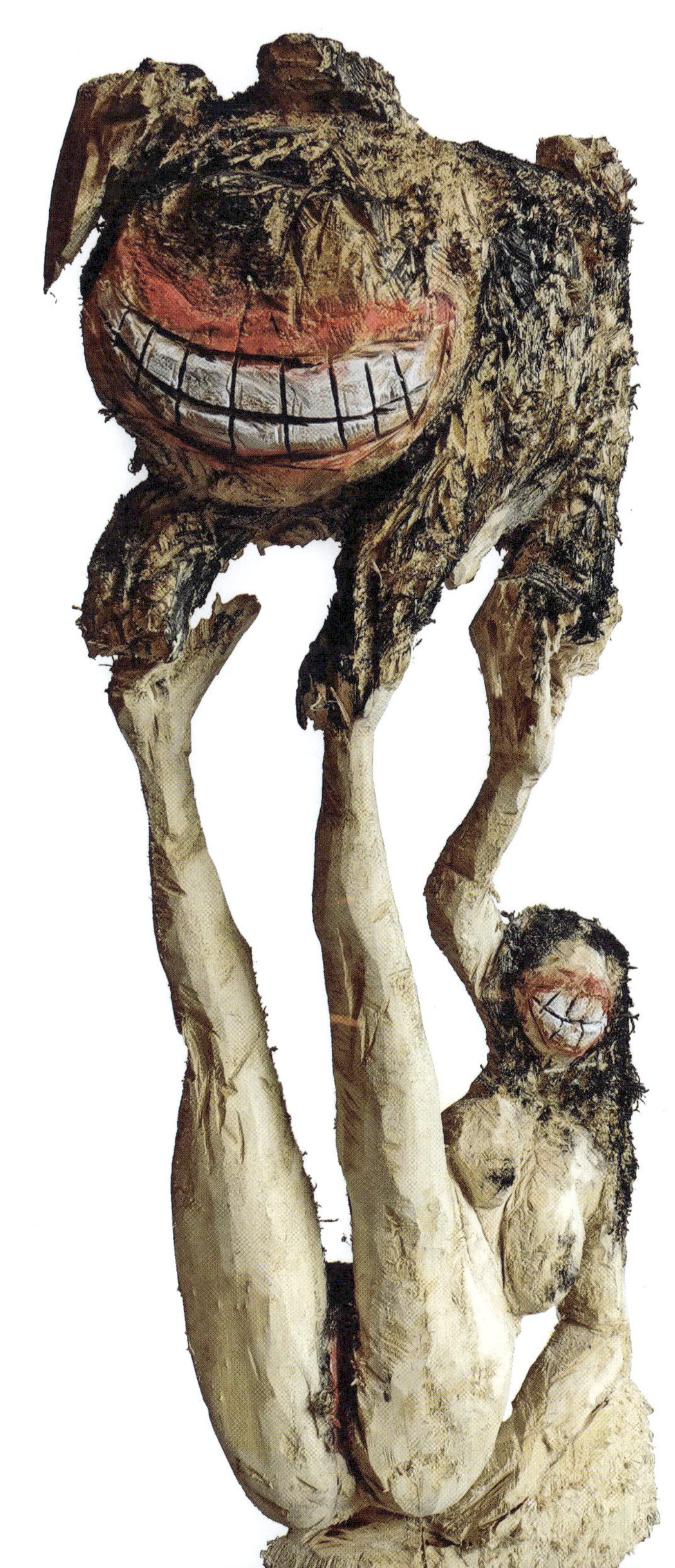

Juli /
July
2016

Ästling

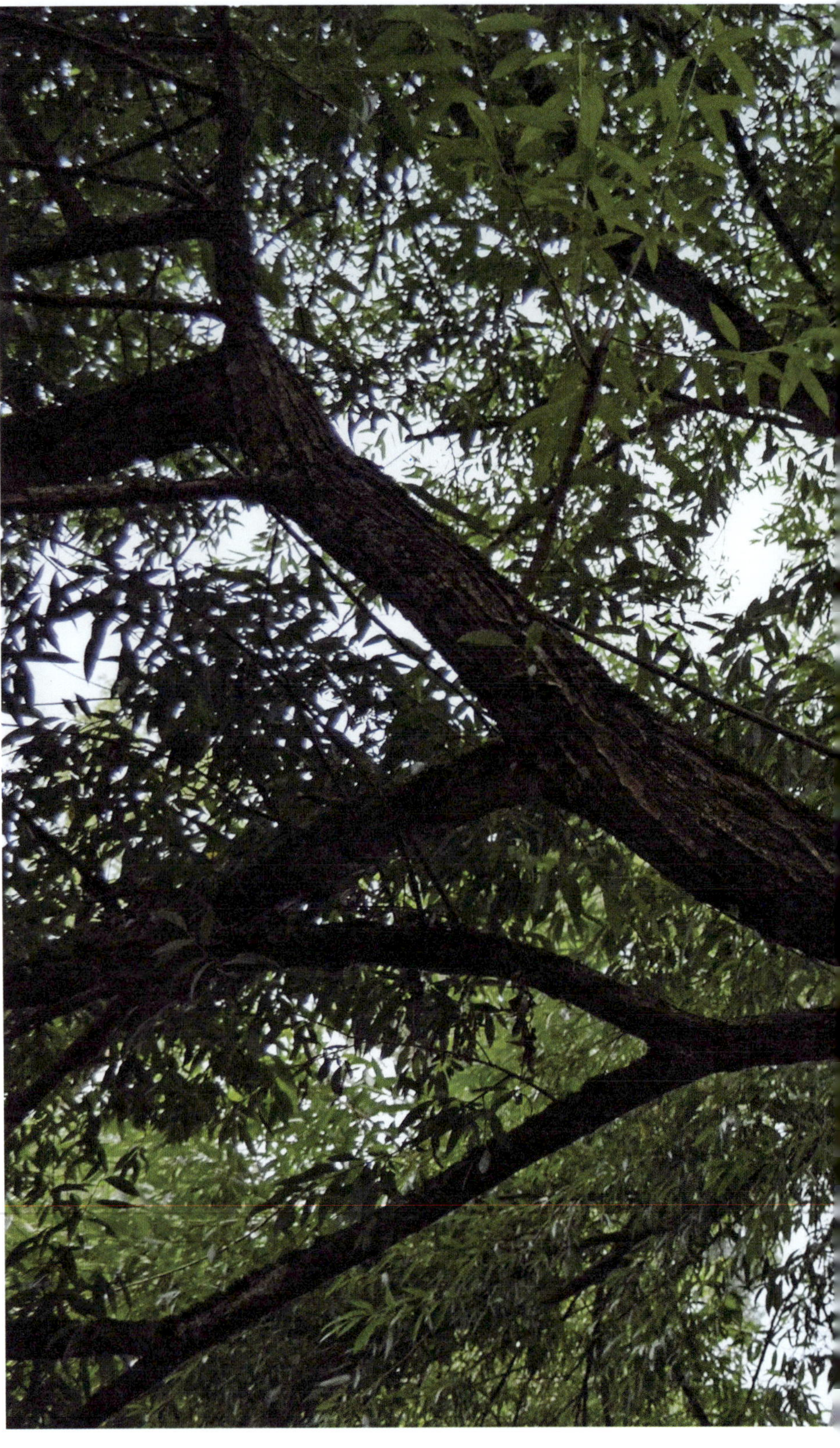

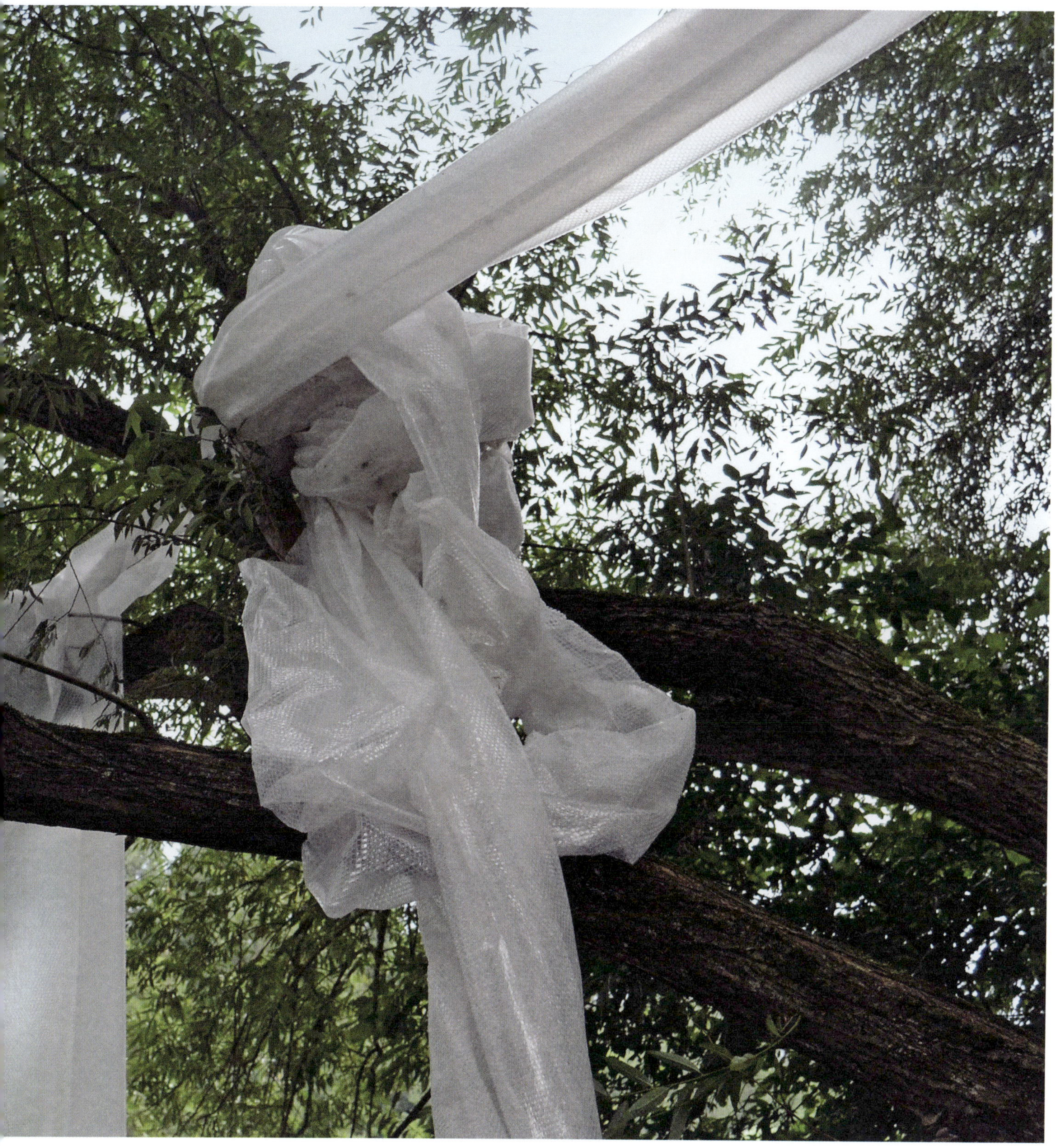

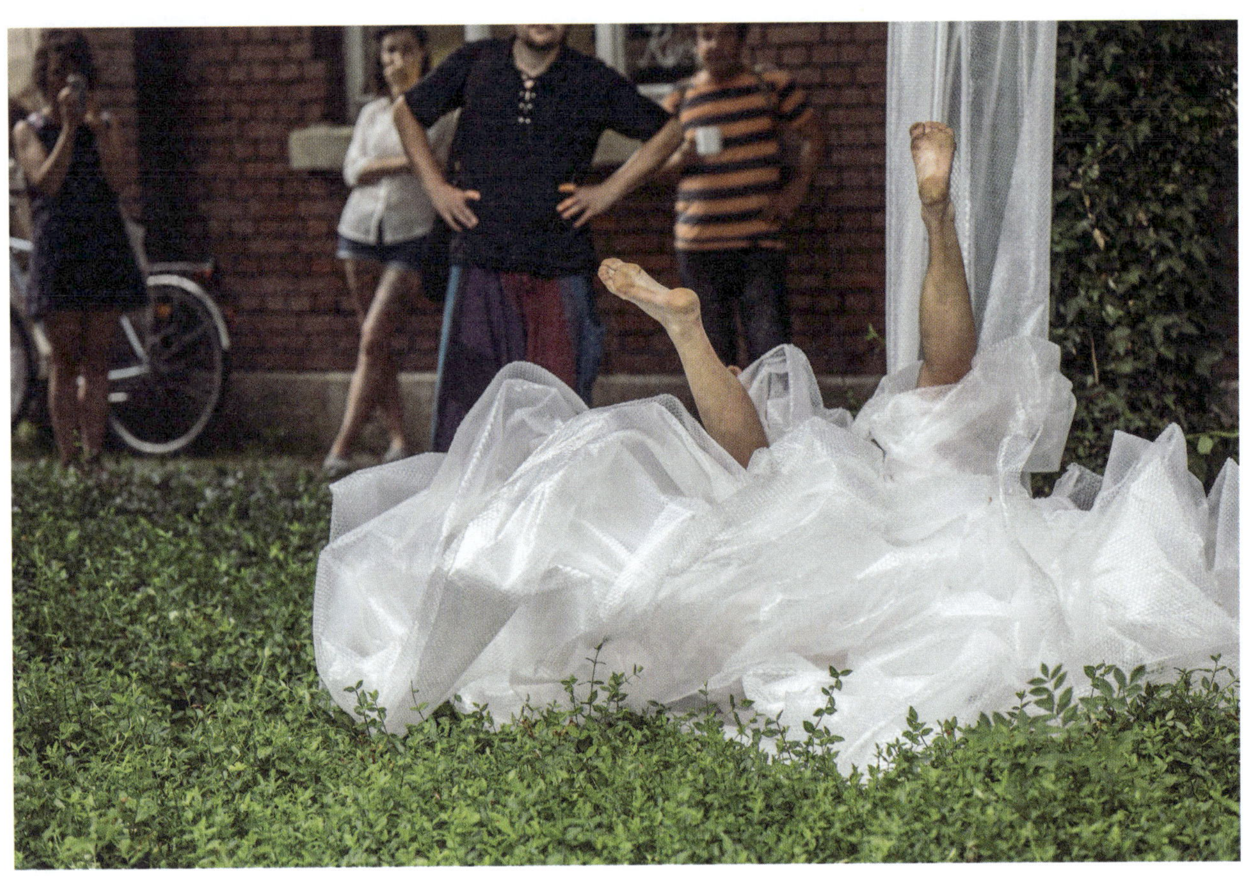

Performance mit Luftpolsterfolie in den Bäumen des Melchiorareals Nürtingen, anlässlich des 40-jährigen Jubiläums der Freien Kunstakademie Nürtingen, 22. Juli 2016. Mit der Performance *Ästling* nahm der Künstler bewusst das Bild des noch nicht ganz selbstständigen Jungvogels auf. Er setzte sich mit der Lebensrealität des aus dem Schutz der Akademie heraus flügge werdenden Künstlers auseinander, die immer ein Balanceakt zwischen Abheben, Scheitern und dem Finden von Wegen darstellt. Die Performance startete in den Räumlichkeiten der FKN und erstreckte sich über eine Stunde lang über das gesamte Areal bis zum Neckar. Wobei der Künstler bei seinen Versuchen, unwägbare Wege zu nehmen, immer wieder auf die Hilfe der Zuschauer angewiesen war (S. 14).

Performance with bubble wrap in the trees of the Melchior grounds at the Freie Kunstakademie Nürtingen (FKN; Independent Academy of Fine Arts) to mark its fortieth anniversary, July 22, 2016. The performance *Ästling* (Nestling) dramatized the image of the not quite independent baby bird. It symbolized the reality of the young artist flying the nest and the safety of the academy—always a balancing act between taking off, failure, and finding one's way. Having started inside the FKN building, the performance took the audience on a one-hour-long journey through the academy grounds to the Neckar river. During his attempts to tackle difficult paths, the artist always had to ask the audience for assistance (p. 14).

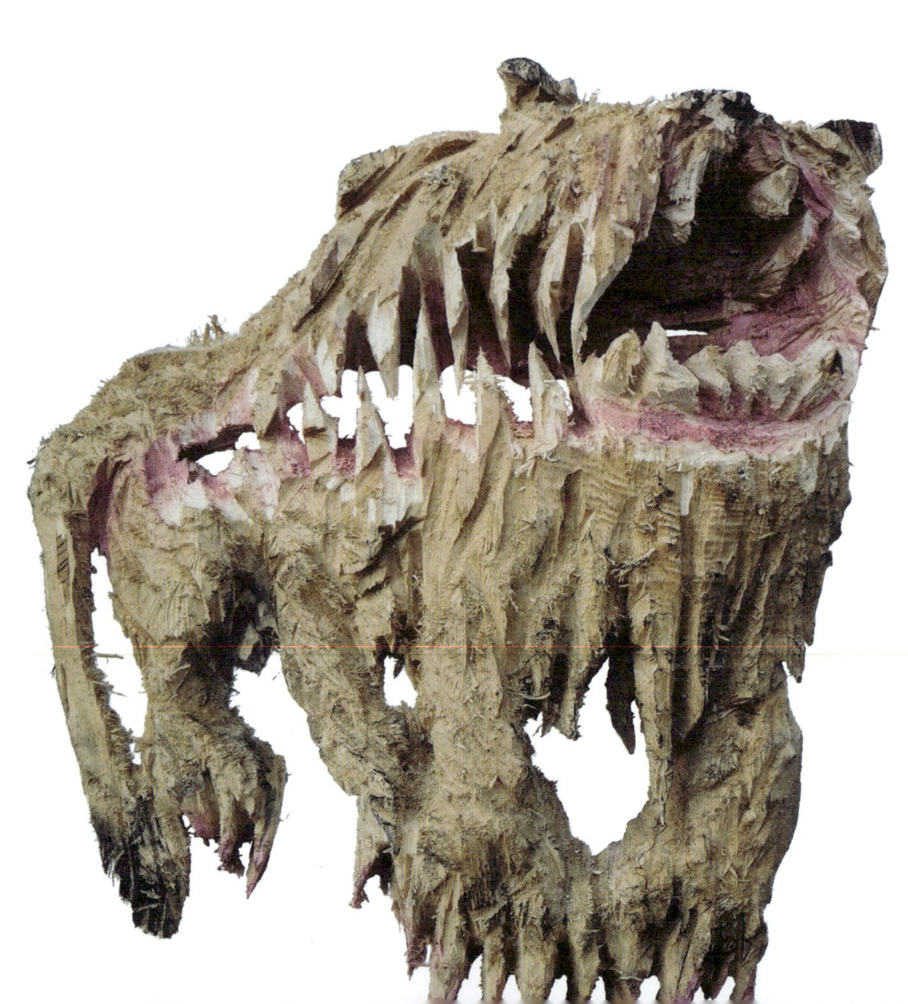

Juni /
June
2014

Passage

Performance mit Tannenzweigen, Plastiktüten und Wurzelschuhen am 4. Juni 2014 (S. 70/71). Zum Ausstellungsprojekt *Transition #2* in der Klettpassage am Hauptbahnhof Stuttgart durchquerte der Künstler im Baumgewand die belebte Einkaufspasse und konfrontierte die überwiegend unfreiwilligen Kunstbetrachter, Reisende und Einkaufende unmittelbar mit der künstlerischen Auseinandersetzung.
Performance with branches of fir, plastic bags, and shoes made from tree roots (pp. 70/71). For the exhibition project *Transition #2*, the artist traversed the bustling Klettpassage shopping arcade at Stuttgart Main Station dressed in tree parts. He encountered the mainly involuntary onlookers, travelers, and shoppers in a direct artistic confrontation.

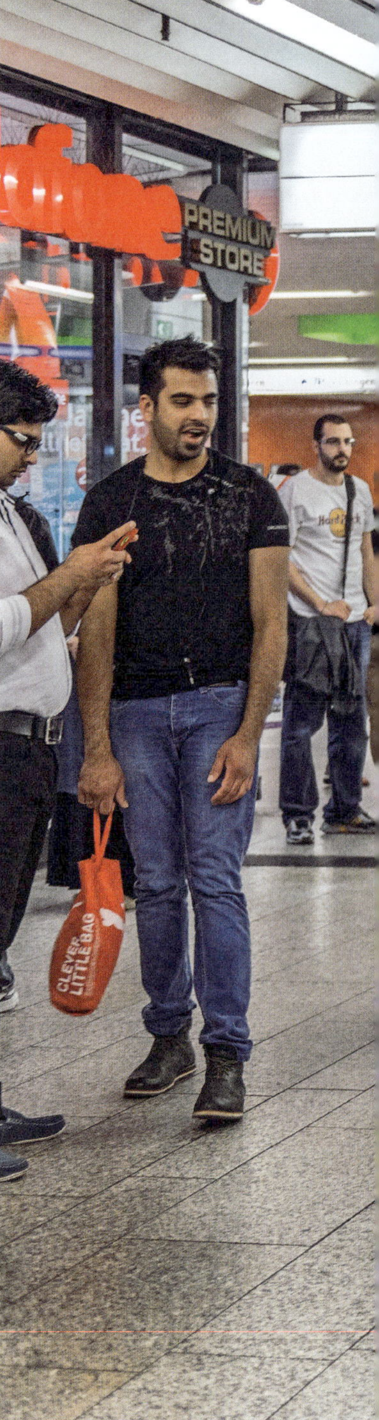

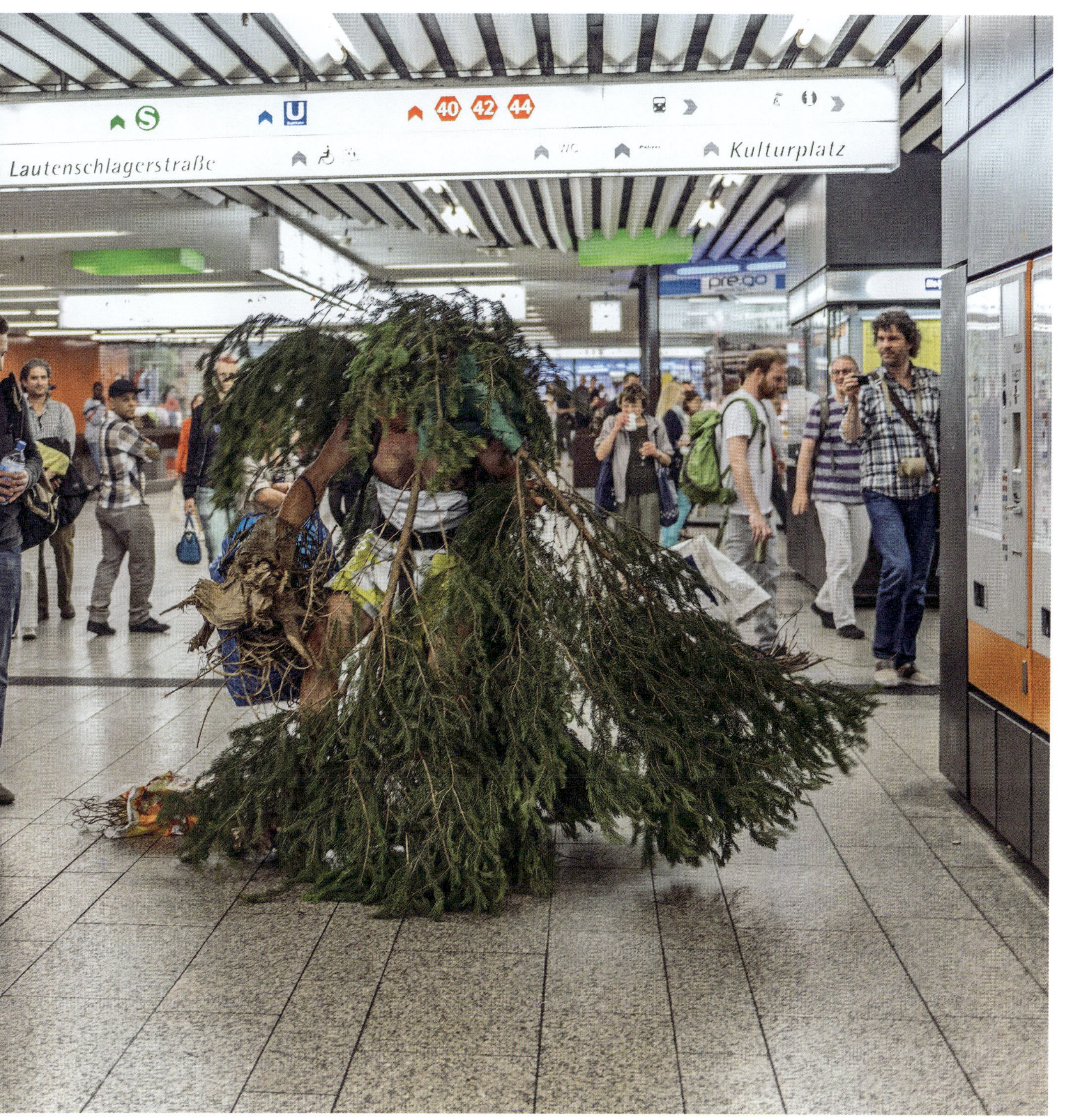
S
U
40 42 44
Lautenschlagerstraße
Kulturplatz
pre.go

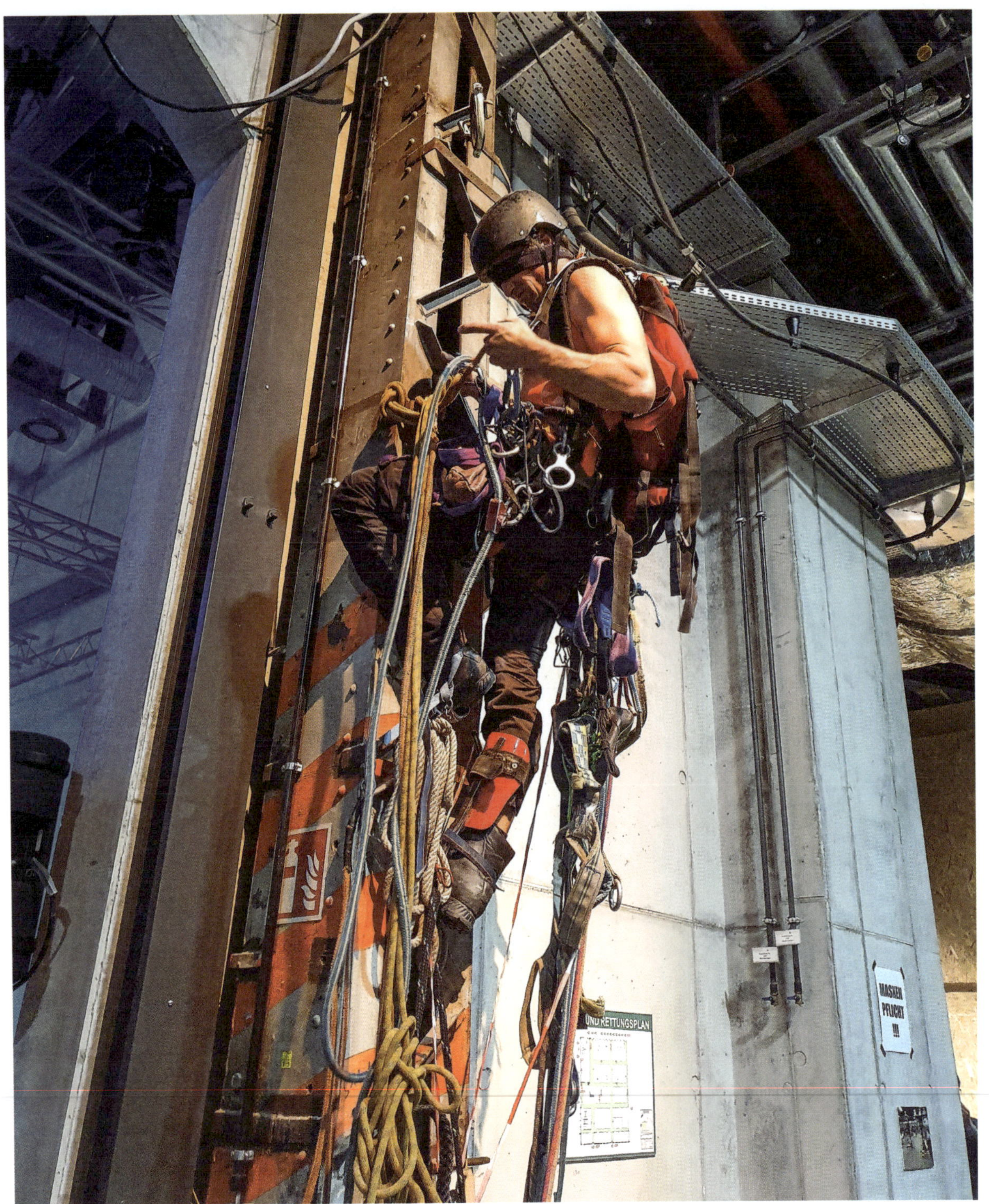
UND RETTUNGSPLAN
MASKEN
PFLICHT
!!!

November 2020

Erstbesteigung Ostpfeiler Wagenhalle

Kletterperformance zur Wiedereröffnung des Kunstvereins Wagenhalle e.V. am 26. November 2020. Der sich blind vorwärtstastende Kletterer hindert sich selbst am Gipfelsieg durch ein Übermaß an Absicherung.
Climbing performance for the reopening of the Kunstverein Wagenhalle e.V., November 26, 2020. Blind and feeling his way forward, the artist impeded his successful climb to the summit with an excess of protective measures.

„Es geht darum, die beste Form für ein unbestimmtes Gefühl zu finden. Die Performance ist dann gelungen, wenn man im Anblick dieser Aktion sich über seine Gefühle und Empfindungen im Klaren ist. Es geht letztendlich um Erhellung.“
“It's about finding the best form for an undefined feeling. The performance is then successful when you are aware of emotions and sentiments while viewing the action. Ultimately it is about enlightenment.”

Thomas Putze

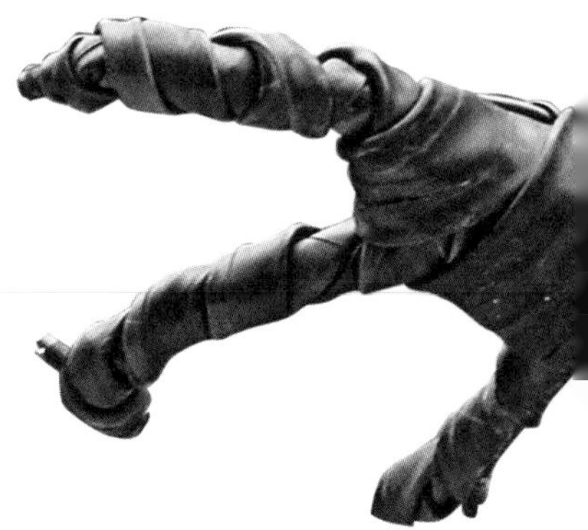

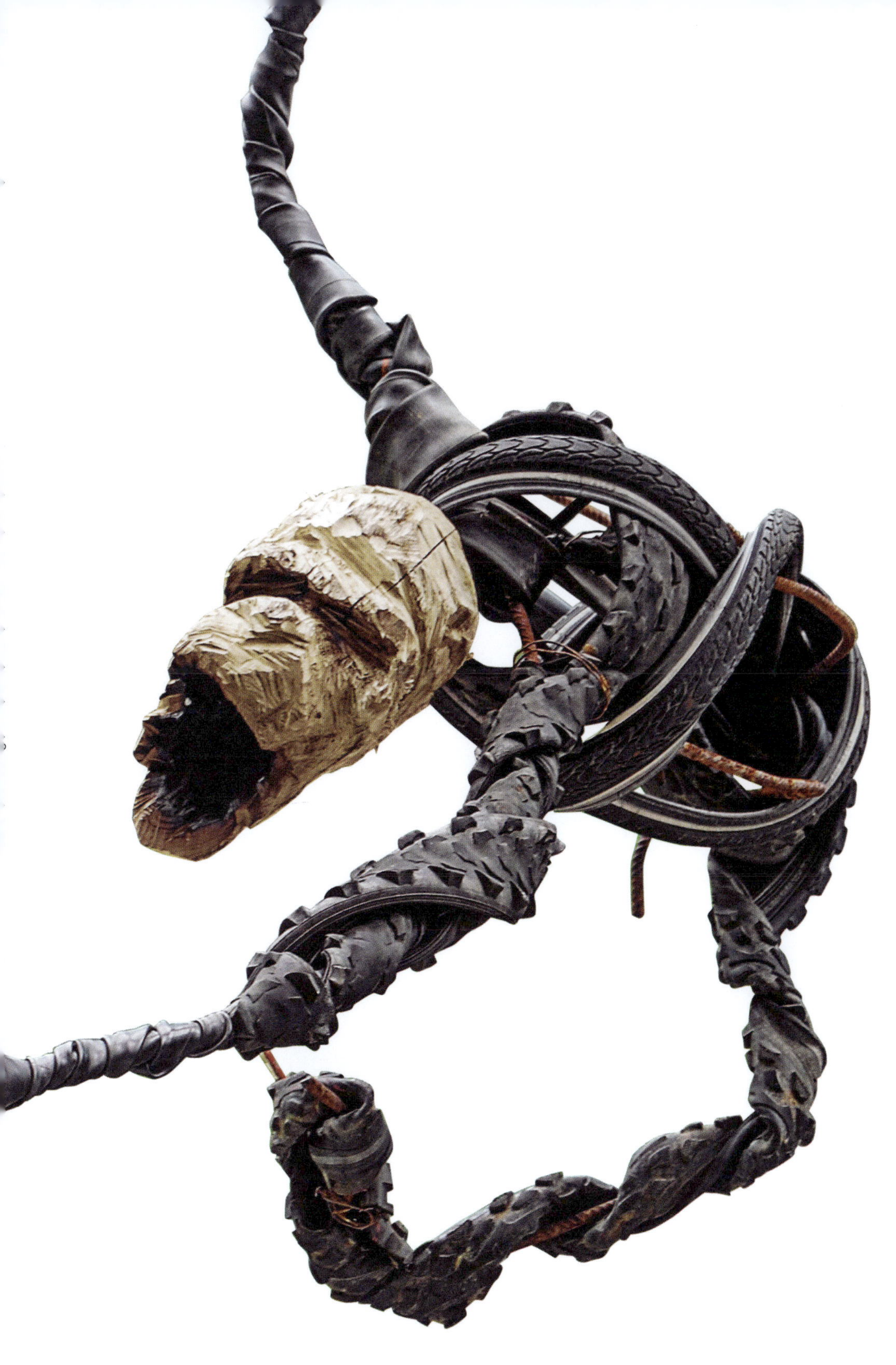

Ein Gespräch in Text und Zeichnung

A Graphic Dialogue

Werner Meyer — Thomas Putze

Kunstwerke, die Welt und im Besonderen die jeweilige Situation in Bildern zu reflektieren und zu interpretieren, ist ein *Kraftakt*, so der Titel der Performance auf der Art Karlsruhe. Zum einen ist die schöpferische Aktion aus dem Atelier an den Ort verlagert, wo es eigentlich um die die Kommerzialisierung der fertigen Produkte geht. „Wie ist das eigentlich gemacht?" ist eine klassische Frage an das Kunstwerk, und als Antwort wird das Narrativ seiner Entstehung mitgeliefert.

Für die Entstehung der anderen, schon fertigen Kunstwerke dürfen wir die Performance als Modell annehmen. Die Entstehung wird in Echtzeit miterlebt, die Betrachter sind Augenzeugen und nicht die die Tat nachträglich rekonstruierenden Detektive. Diese Performance vermittelt auch, dass es einen Kraftakt bedeutet, Bilder zu produzieren, intellektuell, aber auch physisch. Da ist ganzer Körpereinsatz gefordert, oftmals durch das gewählte Material und die eingesetzten Werkzeuge eher noch erschwert, denn erleichtert. Das konterkariert die Leichtigkeit und Selbstverständlichkeit, die die fertigen Arbeiten suggerieren. Das künstlerische Geschehen ein Stück weit transparent zu machen, zumindest als zentrale, wesentlich physische und existenzielle Aktion des Künstlers, scheint mir eine Motivation für Putzes Performances zu sein.

To reflect and interpret artworks, the world, and in particular each respective situation in images amounts to an "act of strength," thus the title of the performance carried out at Art Karlsruhe on February 12–16, 2020. For one, the creative act is taken out of the studio and is in fact transferred to the locus of the finished product's commercialization. "How is it actually made?" is a classic question asked of the artwork—and as the answer, the narrative of its genesis is provided. For the creation of the other, already completed artworks, we may understand the performance as a model. This creating is experienced in real time; the viewers are eye witnesses in real time, not detectives reconstructing an action retroactively. This performance conveys that producing pictures too denotes an act of strength, not just intellectually but also physically. Complete and utter physical exertion is required yet is

Jedes Bild, das Malen, das Bildhauen ist eine Performance, eine ~~spannungsgeladene~~ Aktion mit Spannungsbogen mit Einleitung, Hauptteil und Schluß. Das Erspüren des Endes der Aktion gehört zur Professionalität des Künstlers, das Darüberhinausagieren, das Zuviel ein Unfall aus geistigem Sekundenschlaf.

Als Kunsthistoriker frage ich misstrauisch: Ist das alles, oder zumindest das Wesentliche? Und gleich beginne ich die Zeichen zu deuten, ihre Symbolik zu ahnen, das Theaterhafte der Vorführung zu begreifen und in Verbindung zu bringen zur Unmittelbarkeit und Authentizität des agierenden Künstlers, die Dramaturgie ins Verhältnis zu setzen zur Improvisation, dem Anteil des gelebten und nicht planbaren Moments.

often hindered rather than facilitated by the chosen material and the implements used, counteracting the ease and implicitness that the finished works suggest. Making the artistic process a little more transparent—at least as a central, essentially physical and existential action of the artist—appears to me to be a motivation for the performances. As an art historian I warily probe: Is that all, or the essence at least? And I immediately be-

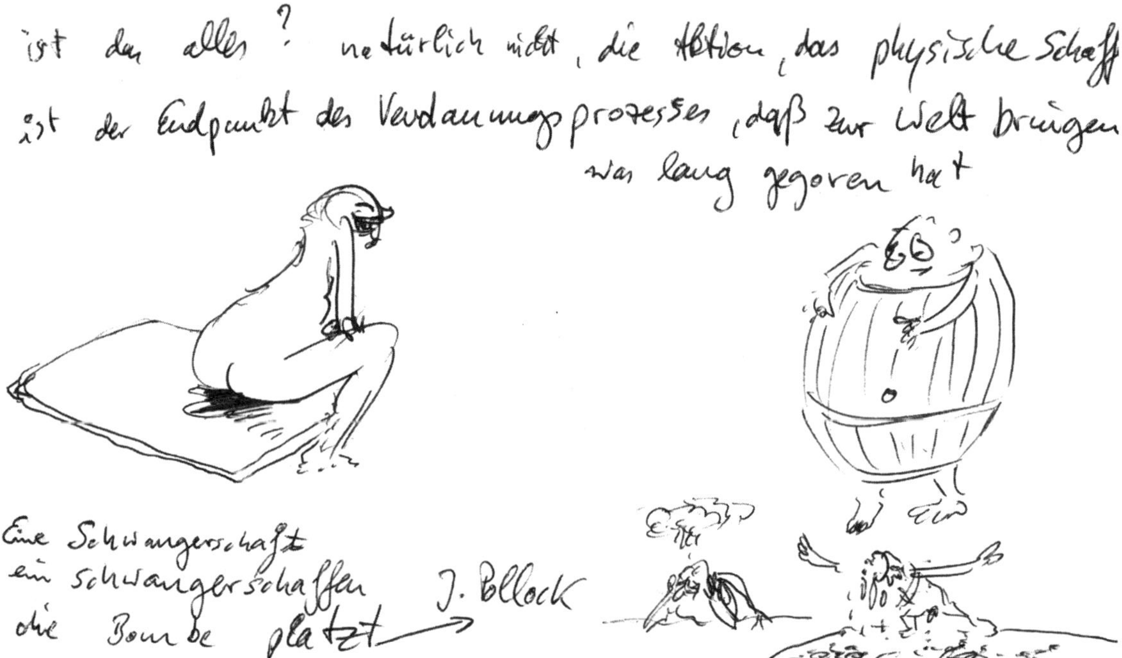

wenn ich denke, denke ich
wenn ich male, male ich

selbst-vergessen, keine Publikumsbeteiligung?
Das Publikum hat gar keine Zeit mitzuschaffen, denn es schafft die Arena, bildet das temporäre Museum für die Dauer der Performance. Das Publikum ist der Dom über dem Knochensplitter des Heiligen
(und der muß noch nicht mal echt sein)

Auch wenn das Publikum dem Künstler so nahekommen darf, so lässt er doch keine unmittelbare Beteiligung zu. Viel eher überlässt er sich einem physischen, selbstvergessenden Einswerden mit seinem Material, mit seiner jeweiligen Umgebung, mit den ihn umgebenden Situationen und jeweiligen Kunstwerken der Ausstellungen und im Besonderen mit den durch die Performances entstehenden Bildern. Die Performances bestehen aus ephemeren, im Moment stattfindenden Bildern, oft bleiben Relikte, die an die Performances erinnern.

gin to interpret the signs, presage their symbolism, grasp the theater-like nature of the performance, and associate the immediacy and authenticity of the artist in action, set the dramaturgy in relation to the improvisation, in relation to the part of the unplanned moment that we experience.
Although the audience may approach the artist, he does not allow direct participation. Rather he gives himself up, physically and obliviously, to become at one with his material, with his respective surroundings, with his locale and the artworks in each exhibition, and in par-

Wiederholung, das serielle, das Gebetsmühlenartige, das Geistige als „stupides" Gehen, Fortgang statt Ideengier.

Wiederkäuen, immer wieder das selbe heißt: es bis ins kleinste zerlegen, es auskosten.

Es entsteht Rhythmus, Einklang

wiederholen = Einüben, das ist Langeweile im positiven Sinn, erst dann versteh ichs.

Nicht selten wiederholt der Künstler im Laufe eines Abends die Performance. Für ein Meisterwerk verbietet sich eigentlich die Wiederholung. Betrachtet man aber die Performance als eine Interpretation der Ausstellung oder eines einzelnen Kunstwerkes, als dessen Reflexion als Dialog, und achtet man auf die Variationen, mit Blick auf die Intensität des Erlebens zusätzlichen Sinn, ein künstlerisches Über- und Fortdenken als Variable des Geschehens.

ticular with the images generated by the performances. These performances are made up of ephemeral images, occurring in the moment, and what often lingers after the performances are vestiges reminiscent of them.

It is not unusual for the artist to repeat the performance over the course of the evening. Repetition is, in fact, forbidden with masterpieces. Yet if one views the performance as an interpretation of the exhibition or of an individual work of art, and its reflection as a dialogue, and if

Warum bleibt der Künstler Thomas Putze nicht freundlich und entspannt im Hintergrund des Eröffnungsrituals und überlässt den Sachverständigen die Informations- und Interpretations-aufgaben, wie sie das Publikum für gewöhnlich erwartet? Will er die Lufthoheit der Interpretation (und des Wissens) für sich beanspruchen und – mit künstlerischen Mitteln – mit seiner Performance das Ritual als Initiierter prägen und in Szene setzen? Die stille Ausstellung ist jedenfalls mit großem Einsatz aufgewühlt. Den Skulpturen und Zeichnungen sieht man natürlich an, wie viel an physischem Einsatz und existenzieller Befindlichkeit ihnen innewohnt. Und man kann die Performance als Teil der Ausstellung, als bewegte Plastik betrachten und erleben. Im Machen und Handeln, in den Themen und Motiven kann man dieselbe künstlerische Sprache und Haltung erkennen. Performance ist Bildhauerei mit anderen Mitteln.

one pays heed to its variations, it gains additional sense in view of the intensity of the experience, an artistic and continual assessment as a variable of the event.

Why is it that the artist Thomas Putze does not remain genial and relaxed in the background of the opening ritual and relinquish the task of providing information and interpretation to the experts, as the public usually expects? Does he want to claim the air of sovereignty over the interpretation (and its knowledge) for himself and, with artistic means, inform and set the scene of the ritual using his performance as the instigator? The calm exhibition becomes actively and purposefully stirred up in any case. One sees in the sculptures and drawings just how much physical exertion and existential sensibility is inherent in them. The performance can be viewed and experienced as part of the exhibition, as a moving sculpture, and the self-same artistic language and mindset

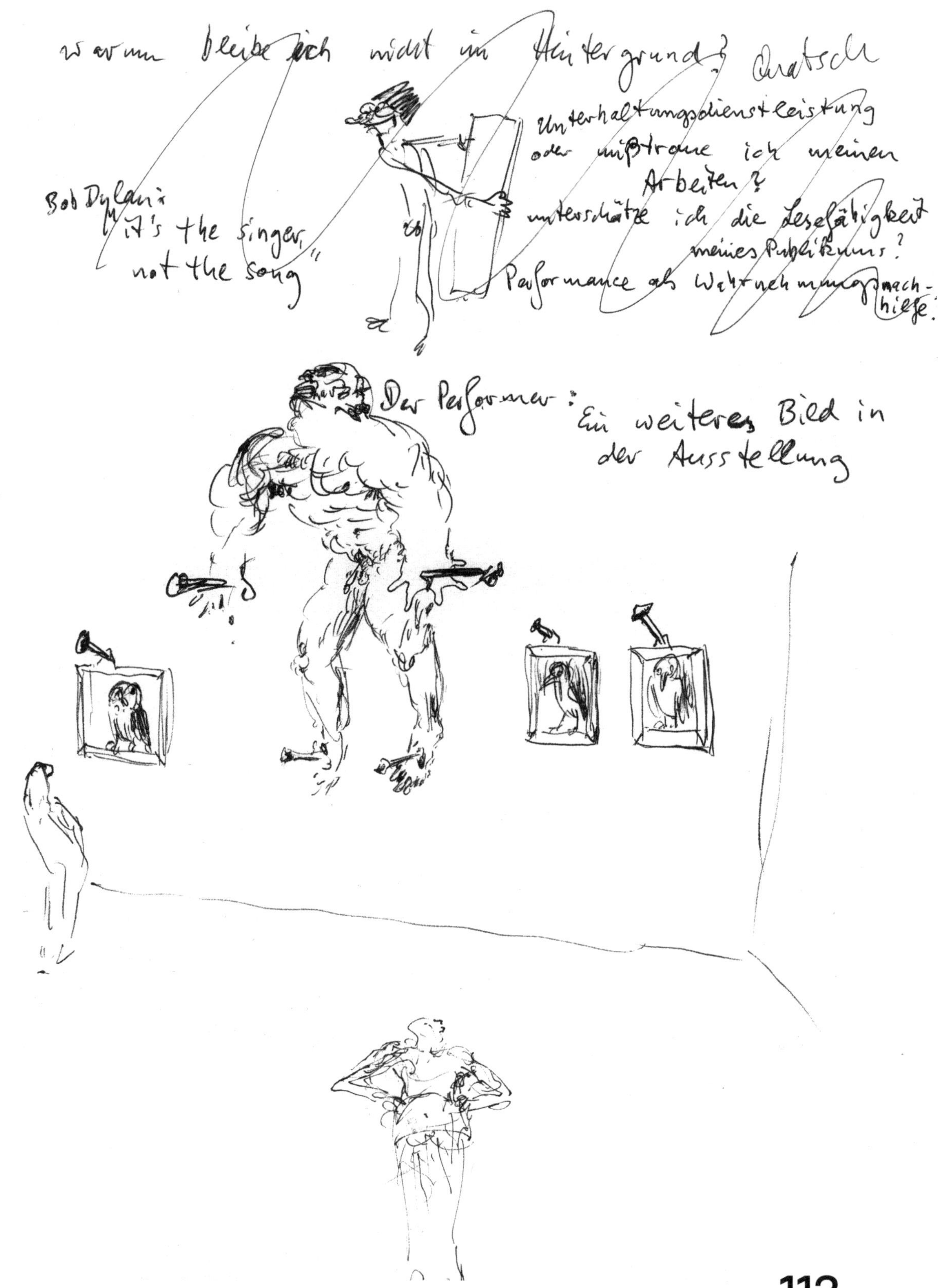
warum bleibe ich nicht im Hintergrund? Quatsch
Unterhaltungsdienstleistung
oder mißtraue ich meinen Arbeiten?
unterschätze ich die Lesefähigkeit meines Publikums?
Performance als Wahrnehmungsnachhilfe.
Bob Dylan: "it's the singer, not the song"
Der Performer: Ein weiteres Bild in der Ausstellung

Eine häufige Begleiterin in den Performaces ist eine seiner Gitarren. Thomas Putze spielt und singt eigene Songs oder interpretiert die anderer Autoren, oder er improvisiert, wobei der Blues häufig den Rhythmus und die musikalische Stimmung bestimmt. Die Songs beschreiben Momente und Stimmungen und verkörpern in der Performance ein weiteres Narrativ, vergleichbar den Material- und Gegenstandscollagen in der Skulptur. Thomas Putze ist auch als Musiker Künstler, mit beeindruckender Virtuosität und starkem Ausdruck. Auch das ist ein plastischer Moment in seiner Performance. In seiner Musik schwingt im Besonderen auch die Melancholie mit, die zu dem Humor und dem clownesken Witz in seinem Werk gehört.

can be seen in the making and action, in the themes and motifs. Performance is sculpture by another means. It is only the object attended to (the material) that is different: the artist's body.

A frequent accompaniment to his performances is one of his guitars. Thomas Putze plays and sings his own songs, interprets those by other authors, or improvises; here the blues frequently determines the rhythm and musical atmosphere. The songs describe moments and moods and embody a further narrative in the performance, comparable to the collages of material and objects in his sculptures. Thomas Putze is also a music artist, with impressive mastery and a strong expression. That too is a sculptural moment in his performance.

You know that I've been on that
big ol' rood so long
thought this live on the street
makes me strong
but I turned out to be a real week man
this lonesome road caused me a lot of pain
did this for a while
but I
won't do it no more, ain't that ahead what
we're looking for?

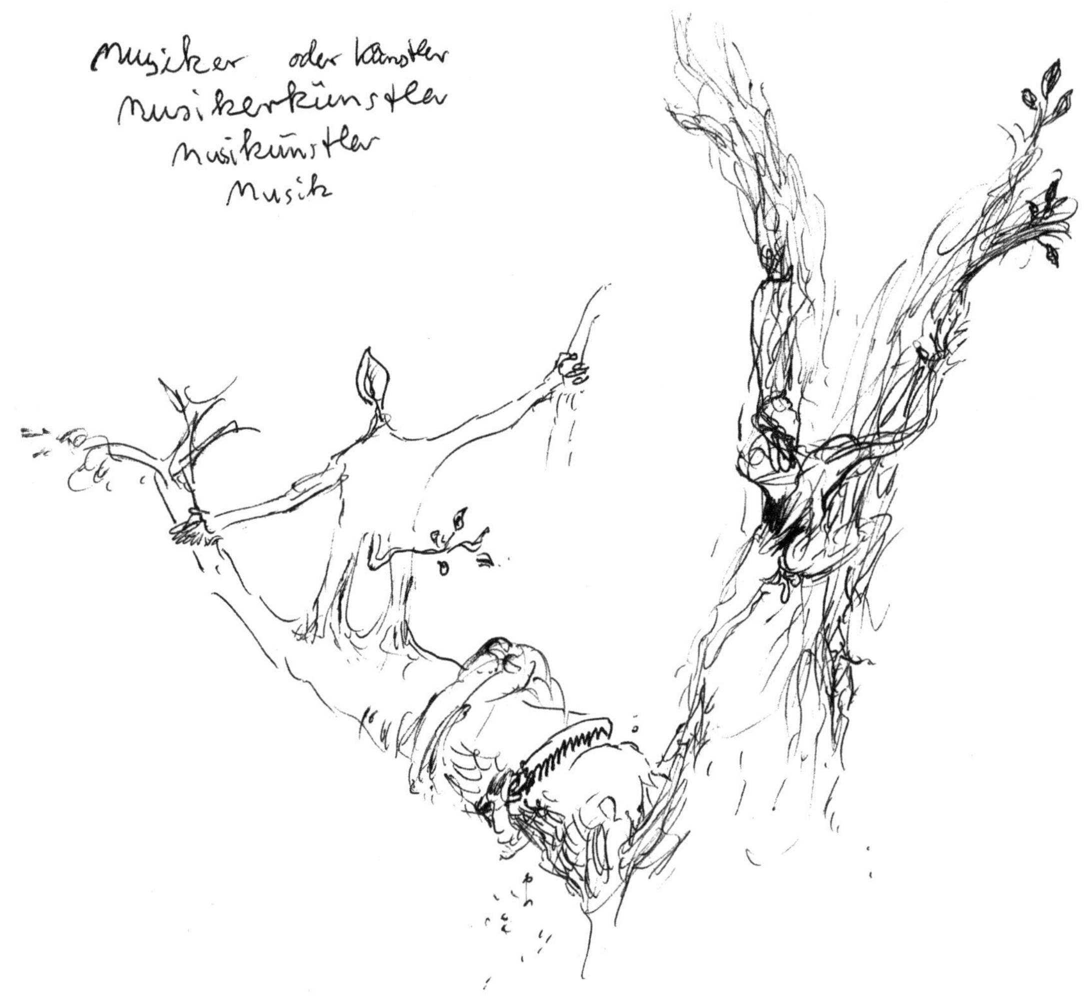
Musiker oder Künstler
Musikerkünstler
Musikünstler
Musik

Thomas Putze ist (auch) ausgebildeter Baumpfleger. Dazu muss er ein geübter und sicherer Kletterer sein. Diese Fähigkeit findet sich in vielen Performances, immer wieder zwischen Himmel und Erde, Boden und Decke des Ausstellungsraumes, an Wänden der Architektur zwischen oben und unten, zwischen Bodenhaftung und schwindelnder Höhe. Wenn man an den Kraftakt denkt, so kann man auch diese Aktionen sinnbildlich verstehen. Das Erklettern ist ein Kraftakt, mit hohem Risiko, und es geht an die Grenzen des Performers, künstlerisch und tatsächlich physisch. Da ist der Künstler dem Hochleistungssportler ähnlich, auch wenn die Wertung des Ziels und Ergebnisses mit völlig anderen Kategorien belegt ist. Mit seinem Klettern eignet sich Thomas Putze den Raum, die Architektur, den Baum performativ an, macht sie zur Skulptur und zum wesentlichen Motiv und Teil seines dynamischen Tableau vivant.

Alongside the humor and clownish wit in his work, melancholy in particular resonates throughout his music.

Thomas Putze is a trained arborist, and for this he has to be a proficient and assured climber. This skill can be witnessed in many performances, repeatedly, between sky and earth, the floor and ceiling of an exhibition space, on architectural walls bound above and below, between down-to-earth and dizzying heights … In thinking about an act of strength, these actions can be understood in a symbolic way. Climbing is a high-risk act of strength, which pushes the boundaries of the performer, artistically and indeed physically. Here the artist is similar to a high-performance athlete, even if the evaluation of his goal and outcome affords completely different categories. When climbing, Thomas Putze takes possession of the space,

Theologe,
Märtyrer:
sterben für
das Leben
Spaß am selbstzugefügtem Leid, dosiertes Leid: ich habe die Kontrolle über das Wehtun, das macht es wohltuend

Und wenn er ein christliches Kreuz erklettert, dem Gekreuzigten leibhaftig ganz nahekommt (Martinskirche, Stuttgart, 2011). Oder, wie an der Schorndorfer Stadtkirche, wo Thomas Putze eine leere Nische an der Außenfassade erklettert und sich in sie stellt – die Leere nach dem Bildersturm neu einnimmt und ausfüllt, nackt und als Camouflage – den Körper mit dem Steinmehl besprüht, wird er zur Steinskulptur wie unbekannte Heilige oder Märtyrer, deren Platz er einnimmt, als Künstler, in einer künstlerischen Performance, Anfang des 21. Jahrhunderts (S. 38–41). Denken ist wie Sprechen eine Handlung, ein Akt – im Bild gedacht als Performance. Thomas Putze ist auch studierter Theologe und er weiß, an welche Grenzen er da stößt. Hätte er eine Portraitskulptur von sich „für immer" in diese Nische gestellt, wäre das wohl eine übergriffige Anmaßung gewesen. In der Performance gilt: Für den Moment genügt die Behauptung. Nach-Denken ist provoziert für eine These, eine Möglichkeit, denn Künstler haben sich in der Kunstgeschichte immer wieder in der Rolle des Schmerzensmanns (Albrecht Dürer) oder der des Märtyrers gesehen, mal ganz abgesehen davon, wie viele Künstler (wie auch Wissenschaftler) tatsächlich Märtyrer für ihre Haltung und für ihre Wahrnehmungen wurden.

architecture, tree in a performative way, turns them into sculpture and into an essential motif and part of his dynamic tableau vivant.

Also when he scales a Christian Cross, verging on the crucified incarnate (Martinskirche, Stuttgart, 2011). Or at the church in Schorndorf, where Thomas Putze climbed up to an empty niche on the outside facade and perched there—juxtaposing himself with and filling the empty space after the iconoclastic incident, naked and camouflaged—his body sprayed with powdered stone as he became a stone sculpture, like the unknown saint or martyr whose place he, as the artist, appropriates in an artistic performance at the beginning of the twenty-first century (pp. 38–41). To think is as to speak; it is an action, one conceived in the image as a performance. Thomas Putze is a graduate theologian too, and as such he knows the boundaries he comes up against. Had he placed a portrait sculpture of himself in the niche "for all eternity," that would have been a transgressive presumption. In the performance, at that moment, the predication is enough. Afterthought provokes assumption, a possibility. For artists have repeatedly seen themselves in the role of the Man of Sorrow (Albert Dürer) or role of the martyr, not to mention the many artists (and scholars) who indeed did become martyrs on account of their attitude and how they perceived things.

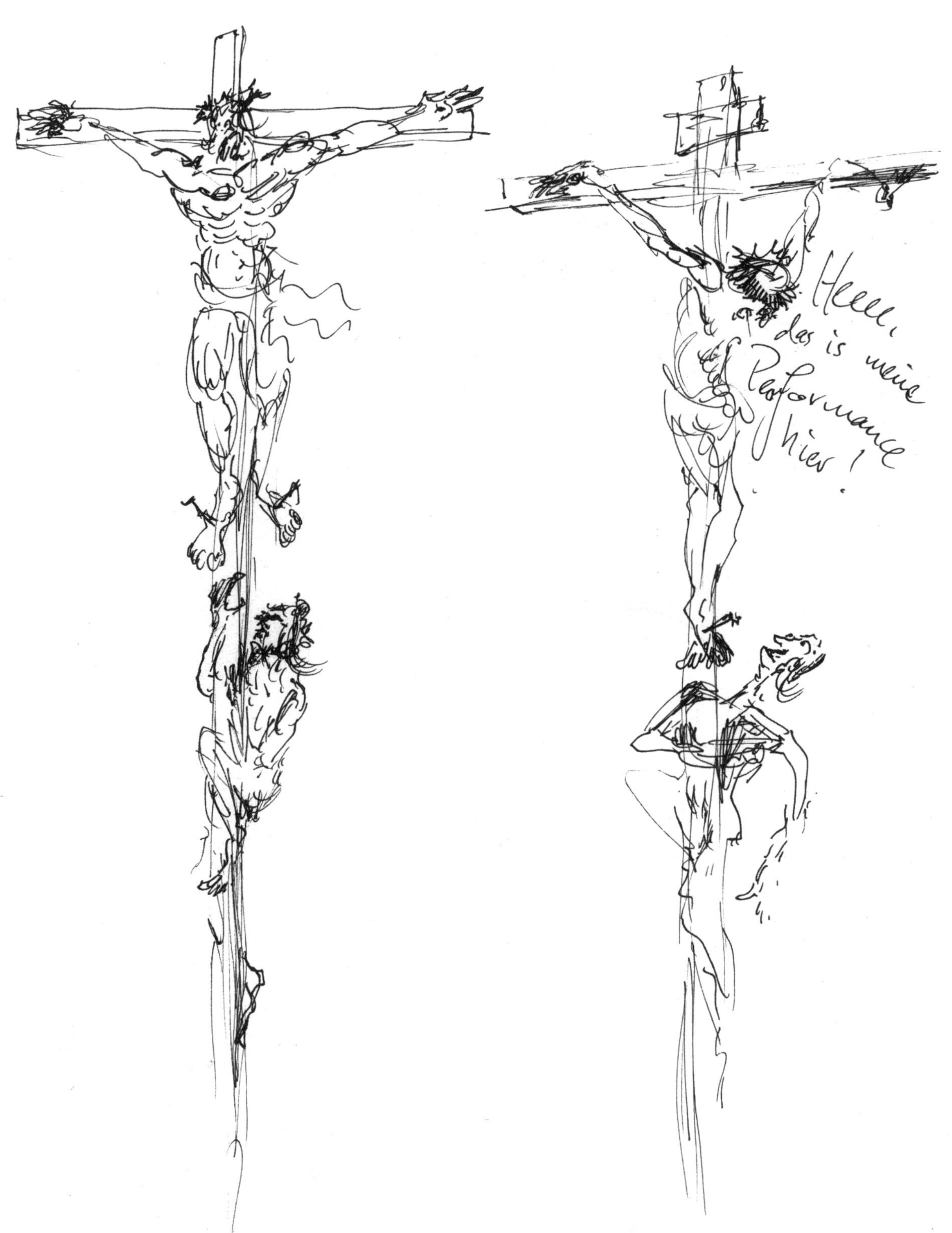
Heeee,
das is meine
Performance
hier!

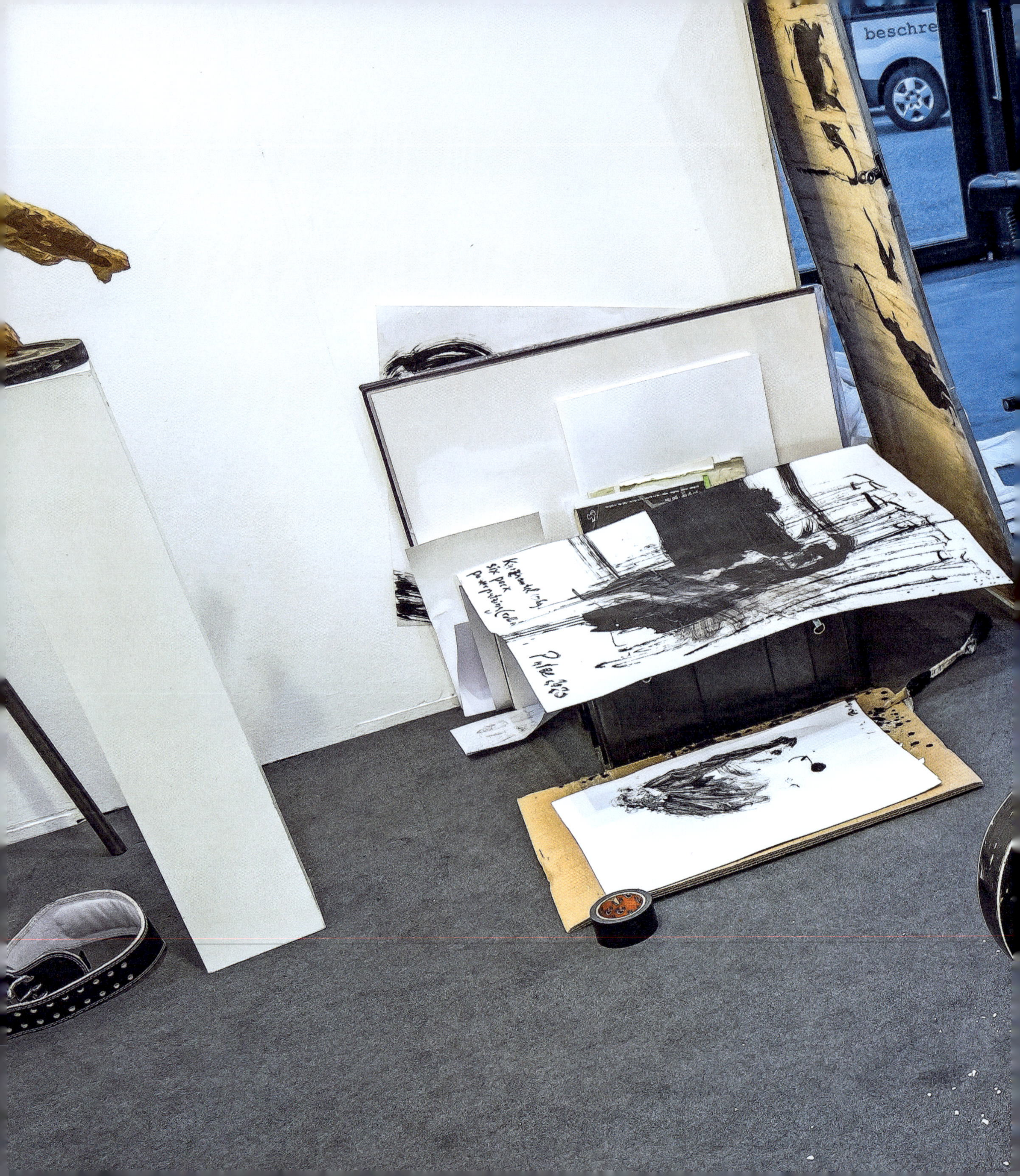
beschre

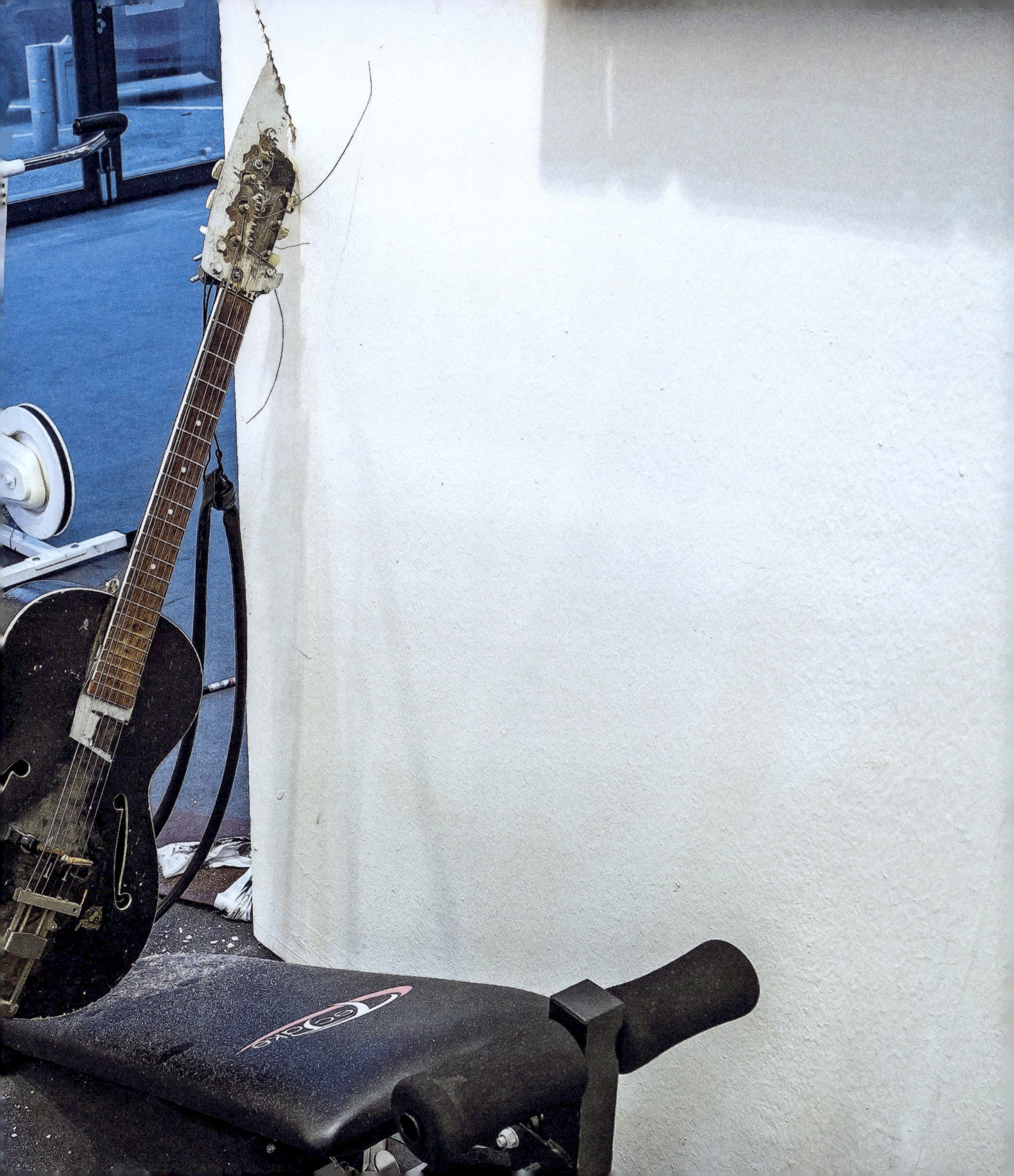

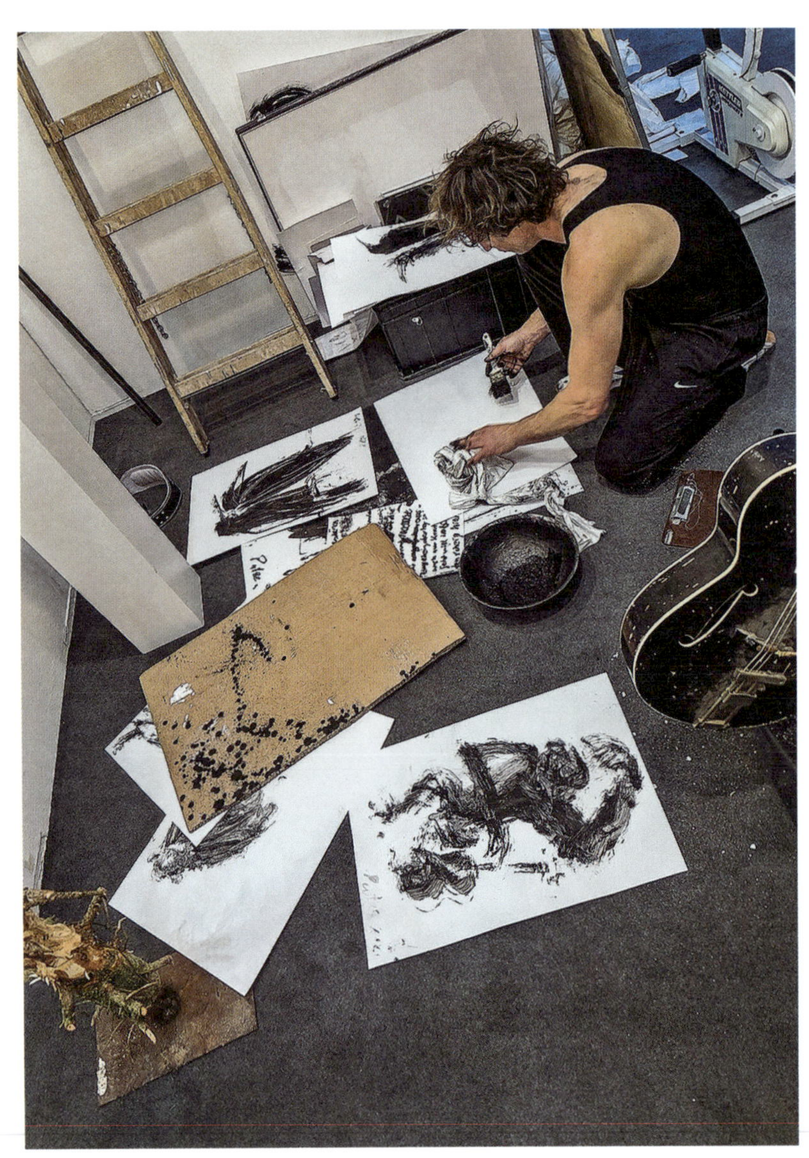

„Das Spektrum der künstlerischen Aktivitäten von Thomas Putze reicht von der Performance, über die Konstruktion von merkwürdigen Gerätschaften, wie etwa einer Spatengitarre […] usw. über Malerei und Bildhauerei bis hin zur Zeichnung […] Thomas Putzes Aktionen fließen aus der Hand und sie sind letztendlich Resultate des Tastens mit dem Stift. Zeichnung das ist der eigentliche Ursprung, das Epizentrum seiner Arbeit.“

“The spectrum of Thomas Putze's artistic activities ranges from performance, via constructing strange apparatus, such as a spade-guitar […] etc., to painting, sculpture, and drawing. […] Thomas Putze's actions flow from his hand; they are ultimately the result of feeling his way with a pen. Drawing—that is the underlying origin, the epicenter of his work.”

Wolfgang Heger

Thomas Putze

07.02.1968	**geboren in Augsburg** Born in Augsburg
1984–1987	**Lehre als Landschaftsgärtner** Trained as a landscape gardener
1990–1991	**Aufenthalt Guatemala, Aufbauprojekt, Entwicklungshilfe** Sojourn in Guatemala, development project, developmental aid
1991–1993	**Theologiestudium in Wuppertal** Studied theology in Wuppertal
1994–1998	**Freiberufliche Tätigkeit als Illustrator und Musiker** Worked as a freelance illustrator and musician
1997	**Studium der Malerei an der FKS in Stuttgart** Studied painting at the Freie Kunstschule in Stuttgart
1998–2003	**Studium der Bildhauerei an der Staatlichen Kunstakademie in Stuttgart bei Werner Pokorny und Micha Ullman** Studied sculpture at the Academy of Fine Arts in Stuttgart under Werner Pokorny and Micha Ullman
Seit / since 2003	**tätig als freischaffender Künstler, Atelier Wagenhallen, Stuttgart** Freelance artist, Atelier Wagenhallen, Stuttgart
2015–2020	**Dozent für Bildhauerei, Performance und Zeichnen an der Freien Kunstakademie Nürtingen** Tutor in sculpture, performance, and drawing at the Freie Kunstakademie Nürtingen

Ausstellungen (Auswahl) / Exhibitions (selection)

2021 *Thomas Putze – Flattermann. Skulptur, Zeichnung und Performance*, Hans Thoma Kunstmuseum, Bernau im Schwarzwald. *Schrittmacher*, Kunstverein, Worms, Skulptur und Performance, Kunstverein, Leonberg. *Blindgänger*, Galerie Schacher – Raum für Kunst, Stuttgart.
2020 *Sculptour 2020* – Beukenhof Phoenix Art Gallery, Kluisbergen, Belgien / Belgium (GA). *Schlangenlinien – Vom Suchen und Finden in der Kunst*, Städtische Galerie in der Badstube, Wangen.
2019 *Thomas Putze außer sich*, Kunstverein, Gütersloh. *Kraftakt*, Rathaus, Stuttgart. *Eden – Brandt, Putze, Welzenbach: Inferno in der Kunst*, Museumsgalerie im Bürgerhaus, Aalen-Wasseralfingen (GA). *Thomas Putze – choppin' thru life. Zeichnung, Skulptur, Platten-Release*, Galerie Peter Tedden, Düsseldorf. Donaugalerie 2019, Projekt der Galerie der Stadt Tuttlingen in Kooperation mit dem Museum Art.Plus, Donaueschingen (GA).

2018 *Thomas Putze – Ausflüge*, Kunstverein, Ludwigsburg. *Myths – Upcycled: Kunst aus Abfall- und Naturmaterialien*, Kunststation Kleinsassen (GA). *Affentheater*, Kunst Forum Rottweil (GA).
2017 *Thomas Putze – Mitspieler*, Galerie Schlichtenmaier, Grafenau. *ArtGenossen – Das Tier und wir*, Städtische Galerie Fähre, Saulgau (GA). *Kleinholz*. Kreuzkirche Nürtingen. *Der Affe und der Ich*, Städtische Galerie, Bad Wimpfen.
2016 *Bildschweine – Malerei und Skulptur – Axel Brandt und Thomas Putze*, Kunstverein Radolfzell e.V. in der Villa Bosch, Radolfzell. *Thomas Putze – ex immunitate: Skulptur, Zeichnung, Performance*, Galerie im DreiGiebelHaus, Xanten. *Thomas Putze – vogelfrei*, Kunstverein, Germersheim. *Band Art Festival*, Galerie Peter Tedden, Düsseldorf (GA).
2015 *Auf dem Holzweg*, Stern-Wywiol Galerie, Hamburg (GA). *Thomas Putze und Piotr Rambowski*, Galerie am Stall, Hude (Bremen). *Jahresausstellung des Künstlerbundes Baden-Württemberg*, Städtischen Galerie, Karlsruhe (GA).
2014 *Höhere und niedere Affen*, Kunstverein, Gelsenkirchen. *Frühblüher*, Lobdengau-Museum, Ladenburg. *3+3 Künstler laden ein*, MEWO Kunsthalle, Memmingen (GA). *Kosmonauten*, Galerien für Kunst und Technik, Schorndorf. *drauf und dran*, Kunstverein, Böblingen.
2013 *Thomas Putze – alles Putze*, Galerie Tobias Schrade, Ulm. *Anschluss*, Goethe-Institut, Nowosibirsk, Russland / Russia. *Die Wagenhallen außer Haus*, Galerie der Stadt Backnang (GA).
2012 *Thomas Putze (Skulpturen, Zeichnungen) – querfeldein*, Galerie am Stall, Hude. *Stammesbrüder*, Städtische Galerie, Ostfildern. *Hauptsache Skulptur*, Galerie Ursula Keller, Mannheim (GA). *aussichtKUNST*, Skulpturenprojekt auf dem Freiburger Schlossberg, Freiburg (GA). *Bildhauer-Zeichnung und Skulptur*, Kunstverein Eisenturm, Mainz (GA).
2011 *Die Letzten. Aktion, Performance, Plastik*, Galerie der Stadt Tuttlingen. *Wilde Tiere*, Edwin Scharff Museum, Neu-Ulm. *Thomas Putze – oben ohne*, Galerie der Stadt Delmenhorst. *Neun Positionen. Stahlskulptur im Südwesten*, Sparkassen-Versicherung Kunstfoyer, Stuttgart (GA). *Durchzügler*, Institut für Kirchenbau, Philipps Universität Marburg.
2010 *Grenzbereiche der Skulptur*, Kunstverein, Ludwigsburg. *Thomas Putze – abfahren*, KUNSTdünger e.V., Skulpturenfeld, Rottweil-Hausen. *Happy End*, Kunsthalle, Göppingen (GA). *Performative Interventionen*. Preisträger der IV. Ellwanger Kunstausstellung, Kunstverein, Ellwangen (GA).
2009 *Thomas Putze – verhundst: Skulptur und Zeichnung*, Galerie Peter Tedden, Düsseldorf. *Tierisch gut!*, Kunsthalle Karlsruhe. *Aus dem Stamm – die Sinnlichkeit des Materials – Holzskulptur heute*, Kunstmuseum Singen (GA).
2008 *Thomas Putze – Skulpturen*, E-Werk, Freiburg. *Tier und Mensch – Remember Abul Abaz. Darstellungen von Elefanten*, Kunst Galerie Fürth (GA). *Aus dem Stamm – die Sinnlichkeit des Materials – Holzskulptur heute*, Kunstverein, Wilhelmshöhe Ettlingen (GA).
2007 *Thomas Putze – Skulptur*, Galerie Peter Tedden, Düsseldorf. *Ritter – Thomas Putze*, Museum am Widumhof, Urbach. *Thomas Putze – Elefantenrunde*, Galerie der Stadt Ostfildern. *Pretty Pets*, Kunsthaus Essen (GA). *Das exponierte Tier – Animalische Koexistenzen*. KISS – Kunst im Schloss Untergröningen, Abtsgemünd (GA).
2006 *Thomas Putze – Sauställe*, Kunstverein Oberer Neckar, Horb a. N. *Vom Pferd erzählen*, Kunsthalle Göppingen (GA). *abgewickelt. Jahresausstellung des Künstlerbundes Baden-Württemberg*, Sulz a. N. (GA). *WG/3ZI/K/BAR – Ein Haus für KünstlerInnen, Gäste, Freunde*, Künstlerhaus Malkasten, Düsseldorf (GA).

2005 *Installalation*, Kunstverein Trossingen e.V., Trossingen. *Kunstsommer*, Kunstverein Oberhausen, Galerie Peter Tedden, Düsseldorf (GA).
2004 *Thomas Putze – „handgreiflich". Installation und Aktion*, Stellwerk, Kulturbahnhof Kassel. *„Affenhaus": Debütantenausstellung*, Staatliche Akademie der Bildenden Künste Stuttgart. *Barockers. Jahresausstellung des Künstlerbundes Baden-Württemberg*, Bad Schussenried (GA). *Bärenjagd*, Skulpturenpark Mörfelden, Walldorf (GA).
2003 *Zi-Zi-Däh – Installation und Performance*, Wilhelmshöhe Ettlingen. *R(a)umklettern*, Kunstverein Shedhalle, Tübingen (GA). *Zeichnungklettern. Jahresausstellung des Künstlerbundes Baden-Württemberg*, Sulz a. N. (GA). *Beziehungsweisen*, E-Halle, Freiburg (GA).
2002 *singled out*, Galerieverein Leonberg e.V., Leonberg. *Antonias Zimmer*, Gedok-Galerie, Stuttgart. *Bis dato unbekannt*, Städtische Galerie, Villingen-Schwenningen (GA). *Germinations 13*, École nationale supérieure de beaux-arts, Paris, Frankreich / France (GA). *Der Berg*, Kunstverein, Heidelberg (GA).
2001 *Das Brot dazwischen*, Kunstaktion und Ausstellung zu Hans Seyffers Kreuzigungsgruppe von 1501 in der Hospitalkirche und vor der Leonhardskirche, Stuttgart (GA). *Niveau*, Klasse Ullman der Staatlichen Akademie der Bildenden Künste Stuttgart, Schloss Solitude, Stuttgart (GA).
2000 *KunstKnast, Gesellschaft der Freunde junger Kunst*, ehemaliges Gefängnis, Baden-Baden (GA). *Roling Stones – Natur und Kunst*, Galerieverein Detmold (GA).

* GA = Gruppenausstellung / group show

Sammlungen / Collections

Staatsgalerie Stuttgart, Stuttgart
Forum Kunst Rottweil, Rottweil
Sammlung LBBW, Stuttgart
Morat-Institut für Kunst und Kunstwissenschaft, Freiburg
Edwin Scharff Museum, Neu-Ulm
Sammlung Kreissparkasse Rottweil, Rottweil
Museum Biedermann, Donaueschingen
Galerie der Stadt Delmenhorst, Delmenhorst
Galerie der Stadt Ostfildern, Ostfildern

Auszeichnungen (Auswahl) / Distinctions (selections)

2012 Erster Kunstpreis der Evangelischen Landeskirche in Württemberg
First Art Prize of the Evangelical-Lutheran Church in Württemberg
2011 Fellowship, Hanse Wissenschafts-Kolleg, Delmenhorst
Fellowship, Hansa Institute for Advanced Study, Delmenhorst
2009 Preisträger Ellwanger Kunstausstellung, Kunstverein Ellwangen e.V
Awardee at the Ellwanger Kunstausstellung (Ellwanger Art Exhibition), Kunstverein Ellwangen e.V.
2004 Landesgraduiertenstipendium des Landes Baden-Württemberg
Post-graduate stipend from the State of Baden-Württemberg
2. Preis Skulpturenpark Mörfelden-Walldorf
2nd Prize, Mörfelden-Walldorf Sculpture Park

Danke Stefan Simon

Danke Katja Simon

Danke Wendy Brouwer

Danke Gretta Garve

Danke Monika Ebertowski

Danke Rita Burster

Danke Daniel Theuring

Danke Micha Ullmann

Danke Volkmar Wywiol

Danke Annett Peckert

DANKE RAPPL

Danke Alf Knecht

Danke Peter Tedder

Danke Christina Dickel

Danke Winfried Stürzl

Danke Kathrin Reeckmann

DANKE Elisabeth Heil

Danke Marko Schacher

Stefan Danke Kraft

Danke Melly Müller

Danke Tobias Schrade

Danke Martina Strilic

Danke Sabrina Zerweck

Danke Benny Ulmer

Danke Markus Niessner

Danke Matthias Gronemeyer

Danke Michael Fiedler und Günter

Danke Katrin Butschell

Danke Werner Pokorny

Danke Nikita Gorbunov

Rolle +

Danke Jan Siegert

DANKE Josh von Staudach

Danke Renate Freter Bongaertz

Danke Hans Theodor Lüpke

Danke! Werner Meyer

Danke Dirk Allgaier

Danke Jürgen Knubben

Danke Thomas Ernl

Danke Marcus Gwiasda

Danke Babette Caesar

DANKE Anna-Maria Ehrmann-Schindlbeck

www.arnoldsche.com

Herausgeber / Editor
Thomas Putze

Autoren / Authors
Dr. Katrin Burtschell,
freischaffende Kunsthistorikerin, ehemalige Leiterin der Freien Kunstakademie Nürtingen
freelance art historian, former head of the Freie Kunstakademie Nürtingen

Prof. Dr. Thomas Erne,
Professor für praktische Theologie, Philipps Universität Marburg
professor of practical theology, Philipps Universität Marburg

Werner Meyer,
Kurator, ehemaliger Leiter der Kunsthalle Göppingen
curator, former head of Kunsthalle Göppingen

Prof. Werner Pokorny,
Professor für Bildhauerei, Staatliche Akademie der Bildenden Künste Stuttgart
professor of sculpture, Stuttgart Academy of Fine Arts

Marko Schacher,
Kunsthistoriker, Leiter der Galerie Raum für Kunst, Stuttgart
art historian, head of Galerie Raum für Kunst, Stuttgart

Zitate / Quotations
Prof. Micha Ullmann,
Professor für Bildhauerei, Staatliche Akademie der Bildenden Künste Stuttgart
professor of sculpture, Stuttgart Academy of Fine Arts

Wolfgang Heger,
Leiter Kunstvermittlung des Kunstmuseums Moritzburg, Halle
head of art education, Moritzburg Art Museum, Halle

Konzeption und Redaktion / Concept and editing
Dr. Katrin Burtschell

Übersetzung / Translations
Wendy Brouwer

Grafische Gestaltung / Graphic design
niessnerdesign GmbH, Stuttgart

Offset Reproduktion / Offset reproductions
Paladin Design- und Werbemanufaktur, Remseck

Druck / Printed by
edica, Poznań

Papier / Paper
120 g/m² Magno Natural

Projektkoordination / Project coordination **arnoldsche**
Greta Garle

Bibliografische Information der Deutschen Nationalbibliothek
Die Deutsche Nationalbibliothek verzeichnet diese Publikation in der Deutschen Nationalbibliografie; detaillierte bibliografische Daten sind im Internet über www.dnb.de abrufbar.
Bibliographic information published by the Deutsche Nationalbibliothek
The Deutsche Nationalbibliothek lists this publication in the Deutsche Nationalbibliografie; detailed bibliographic data are available on the Internet at www.dnb.de

ISBN 978-3-89790-624-2
Made in Germany, 2021

Bildnachweis / Photo credits
Katrin Burtschell: S. / pp. 14, 16/17, 32, 94/95
Beate Freier-Bongaertz: S. / pp. 82/83
Reiner Fritz: S. / p. 31
Galerie die Stadt Tuttlingen: S. / pp. 78–81
Marcus Gwiasda: S. / pp. 86/87
Wolf Nkole Helzle: S. / p. 68
bildhübsche fotografie, Fabrice Weichelt: S. / pp. 13, 100/101
Jan Liesegang: S. / pp. 28/29
Andreas Linsenmann: S. / pp. 88/89
Jörg Mandernach: S. / p. 102
Anett Reckert: S. / p. 22
Marko Schacher: S. / p. 48
Antje Schröder: S. / pp. 24–27
Joachim Schüler: S. / pp. 74–76
Josh von Staudach: S. / pp. 4/5, 8/9, 38/39, 41, 46/47, 120–122
Daniel Theuring: S. / pp. 34, 37
Robert Thiele: S. / pp. 90/91
Benny Ulmer: S. / pp. 60–67
Dirk Unkelbach: S. / pp. 15, 96

Umschlagabbildungen / Cover illustrations
vorne / front: *Unterirdisch* (Underground), 2019; **hinten / back:** *Säulenheiliger* (Stylit), 2017